*Praise for* Nancy Fisher's

# Healing Trauma Through Loving Relationships

Childhood trauma is a difficult and painful reality. But Nancy Fisher's book provides solid biblical principles and engaging stories to create a path that works. One of my favorite things about this book is that it encourages the reader to take action sooner rather than later. It is much more effective to heal childhood trauma *when the child is still a child*. Highly recommended.
        --John Townsend, Ph.D. Best Selling Author of *Boundaries*, Psychologist and Leadership Coach

Nancy Fisher illuminates life as a foster family, providing valuable insight to raising and healing children through foster parenting. *Healing Trauma Through Loving Relationships* demonstrates how foster parenting is both a calling and a profession that is vital to the child welfare system.
        --Christina Morrison, Executive Director Indiana Foster Care and Adoption Association

Nancy and her husband, Jim, have been foster and adoptive parents for over 30 years. I have watched this journey unfold, through the ups and downs and watched as Nancy has worked to learn the best ways to love and care for all children. As a therapist who works with foster/ adoptive parents, I have listened as they have also struggled to learn how to love their children and help them heal. This book is a very readable, practical, and understandable guide for those parents who only want to love the most wounded of children. I recommend it for professionals and foster/ adoptive parents who want to understand the children they seek to help and have more ways to do so.
        --Lisa Medanic, L.C.P.C.

We have all heard of unconditional love. By sharing her experiences in this book, Nancy has given us examples of how this gift can benefit those who have been through childhood trauma. Her gifts of unconditional love have enabled her to provide many hopeful futures, both now and generations to come.
    --Jacqueline Cox, Foster and Adoptive Parent

Beyond the pages of this book lies an extraordinary story of what determination, commitment, and triumph looks like. I laughed, I cried, but more importantly I cheered, Yes! Finally someone gets it. *Healing Trauma Through Loving Relationships* paints a complete picture of what can be when we stay committed to the process. Thanks to Nancy, we now know there is Hope.
    --Lisa S. Hubbard, MSW, LSW, Student Services Coordinator, IU School Of Social Work

Fisher does a masterful job of taking the reader into the world of foster care as only a person on the inside can do. This book is a must read for foster and adoptive parents and those who are contemplating parenting children from the public child welfare system.
    --Dr. Gail Folaron, Professor Indiana University School of Social Work.

# Healing Trauma Through Loving Relationships:

## Hope for Foster and Adoptive Families

Nancy L. Fisher

with Megan Kruse

Copyright © 2014 Nancy L. Fisher

All rights reserved.

# DEDICATION

My inspiration for this book comes from my amazing daughter-in-law, Danielle. She is a shining example of a closely attuned parent, connected and attached to my grandson. As I watch her pace herself to join him in his little world of exploration, I am astounded by the incredible experiences that she and my grandson create together. Their relationship is a joy for me to witness, and I have learned much from her.

# TABLE OF CONTENTS

Acknowledgements  8

Preface  9

1. Eric's Story: Creating Essential Attachment  13

2. The Knife in the Kitchen: Being Aware of the Source of the Trauma  35

3. Louis's Story: The Significance of Loss  53

4. The Relationship or the Battle?: Building Attachment Through Intention & Unconditional Love  67

5. Interdependent Living  81

6. Through a Trauma Lens: Toward a New Paradigm for Working with Traumatized Children  93

References  111

About the Authors  113

# ACKNOWLEDGMENTS

    Fostering and adoption are family endeavors, and would not have been possible for me without the tenacious support of my incredible husband, Jim, and our children. In addition, our support system included and continues to include my sisters, our church family, and Grandma, who is everyone's Grandma. I am thankful for all of them.

    I am also grateful for my niece, Megan Kruse, who has patiently helped in the writing of this book. Her gifts of writing and encouragement have made the journey of writing this book a great joy.

# PREFACE

Mary met David in college, where she was studying sports medicine. David was in the teaching program, hoping to eventually work as a science teacher in an underprivileged high school. Mary noticed David's kindness immediately, and he was taken by her contagious laugh echoing through the university's halls. By the end of their sophomore year, they were engaged; the following spring, they married at the church in Mary's hometown.

Both Mary and David had always dreamed of having large families. They were nurturers and healers at heart, and together they imagined their family growing to four or even five. The women in Mary's family struggled with serious fertility issues, and Mary had watched many of them go down heartbreaking paths of failed pregnancies. From an early age, Mary instead imagined opening her home and heart to children in need, and building her own family through adoption. David, meanwhile, had always wanted to foster. His teaching work invigorated him; he felt a personal and spiritual commitment to working with youth, and felt like he had more energy to give outside of the classroom. By the time they were three years out of college and feeling settled in their careers, Mary and David felt that they had the resources to provide for others. They had also just bought their first home with the help of David's parents—a two-story, five-bedroom home on a ten-acre plot outside of town. They had so much, and they imagined and hoped that they could share it with many foster children, and eventually grow their family permanently through adoption.

*Preface*

Eight months later, Mary sat on the sofa, across from the foster care social worker. David helped the boys—two brothers, five and nine, whom they had been fostering for several weeks—into their jackets, and the three of them headed outside to play. When David and the boys were out of earshot, Mary began to cry. "I'm so overwhelmed," she said. "I thought we could do this, but I don't know." She covered her face with her hands. "This was our dream," she said. "And now, we're just discouraged." She reached for a tissue. "I thought this was what we were supposed to do," she said. "But now I don't know. I don't know if we can. I don't know *what* to do."

*Overwhelmed. Discouraged.* When foster/adoptive parents seek out services, these emotions weigh heavily on them; the needs of their child have become engulfing. The child's extensive needs, lack of reciprocal relationship skills, and acting-out behaviors have created a vortex in the home, much like being caught in a perpetual and destructive storm of ongoing and amplifying trauma. They have succumbed to the trauma vortex.

In my nearly thirty years of experience as a foster/adoptive parent, and my twenty-four years of work with other foster/adoptive parents, my heart has often grieved for the pain I see in these families. These are people, like Mary and David, who enter the foster care and/or adoption process with great enthusiasm and positive, loving motives—a desire to grow their families, to make a difference, and to share some of their boundless love with hurting children. Often, however, by the time the family seeks services, these well-meaning parents are exhausted. They are at the ends of their proverbial ropes, ready to give up. To the professionals encountering weary parents for the first time, these once-positive people appear angry, over-reactive, and irrational. Seen through the trauma vortex, we often look warped and ugly. The positive intentions which led parents to adopt are hardly visible in the storm.

That transformation from one extreme to another—from positive enthusiasm to crushing, exhausted defeat—takes place because of the experience of vicarious trauma. The foster/ adoptive parents bring a child into their home who has experienced significant and complex trauma, and this trauma is displayed in out-of-control behavior, defiance, destruction, self-harm, aggression—and the list goes on.

As a foster/adoptive parent, a professional in the field of foster parenting and adoption, and now as a therapist and trainer, I have met hundreds of foster/adoptive parents who have told me their stories. By some measures, I myself have experienced greater "success" in my home with foster and adoptive children than other foster/adoptive parents. If success is defined by the absence of holes in the walls, then we have by no means succeeded. But if you define success by helping children break the foster care cycle through attachment, then our home *has* been successful. That kind of meaningful, life-changing attachment—attachment powerful enough to end the trauma vortex for the next generation—is the reason behind this book. I hope that our stories and hard-won knowledge will be a catalyst for greater attachment, more love, and powerful healing.

So how did we, and how do we, continue to care for and love other people's children for so many years? My mantra has always been to respond to the needs expressed through behavior, rather than reacting to the behavior itself. Over the last thirty years, research on the effects of trauma on the brain has begun to demonstrate more and more clearly that a trauma-informed care approach like this is what works for children who have experienced trauma.

This book is an attempt to explain the research and put it into practical terms through the stories of the children who have lived in our home and been part of our family. I hope that in these chapters, you will find stories that resonate with your own experiences, as well as practical strategies for building attachment, healing trauma and loss, and building sustaining relationships over time and generations. I believe in the potential for trauma-informed care and attachment-based practices to shape a new system, one that works. My hope is that the stories of our experiences, intertwined with research, will benefit foster/adoptive families, as well as all of the friends, family, professionals, and systems which support these remarkable families. My hope is for the Marys and Davids, for the people in their communities and the children they love. Throughout this book I use

*Preface*

the singular *he/him* as default pronouns, a decision I made for simplicity's sake and because Jim and I raised so many sons. Names have been changed to protect privacy, but these stories have been my life, and these kids have been and continue to be my heart.

Nancy L. Fisher

Spring 2014

# CHAPTER ONE

ERIC'S STORY: CREATING ESSENTIAL ATTACHMENT

It was a bitterly cold Thursday in early 1992 when Eric came into our home with his older brother, Alex. Eric was six, slight and blonde; Alex was twelve, sturdier and with dark hair. Because of Alex's behaviors, the two had been moved five times over the course of two years in the system. Their circuitous, unstable path had led them from an emergency foster home to their maternal grandparents' home; from there, they went on to spend six months in a county foster home, then six months in another; finally, they came into our home. We were designated as a therapeutic placement, due to our willingness to take children with more presenting issues, often adolescents. The therapeutic designation meant that we also had the additional weekly support of a case manager from the community mental health center. In other words, Eric and Alex had been escalated to our home, after and because of a bumpy road of failed placements. We hoped to keep them stable and safe for just a few months before they reunited with their birth father. Helping little Eric over the late-winter ice and into our ranch house in Indiana, I had no way to know that this relationship would be transformative for both of us.

Now, more than twenty years after that February afternoon, Eric and I sit talking in a rental condo during a family trip to Disneyworld. Our family is vast and scattered now, but we prioritize time together, and this year we have all descended on Florida together. Multiple generations of core family wander the theme park. Some of us wear rakish mouse ears; some of us are weighed down with backpacks of snacks and water. We stop so the youngest granddaughter can pose for a photograph with a Disney princess she worships. Eric has joined us with his young wife and his child. His son and namesake, "Little Eric," is a sturdy toddler who looks exactly like his father but has experienced a vastly different first two years.

Attachment and trauma are not isolated events, and neither will our discussions of them be. There are different kinds of attachments and detachments, but every child who comes into the foster care system has attachment issues, because every child in the system has experienced profound losses. In other words, I might talk about attachment through the lens of a hundred other children or a thousand other experiences. I choose to tell Eric's story because of how we approached attachment with this young man who would become such a definitive part of my heart and our family. Fostering attachment has been a part of my entire history in this field and as a parent, but with Eric, every moment was intentional. My experiences with Eric were an immeasurably significant part of solidifying my understanding of attachment and my approach to foster and adoptive children.

Here is Eric today: tall and strong, determined, lifting his son onto his lap. Speaking now of the last twenty years, what strikes me most is my hand, touching his shoulder as we talk, and everything that touch symbolizes between us—the careful, deliberate gestures of love and security that build attachment.

## *The Brain, Needs, and the Roots of Attachment*

To fully understand the impact of childhood trauma, it is essential to understand the brain. In the nineties, scientists began to turn their focus on the brain, and the last twenty years of research have provided significant new knowledge about how this exceptional organ works. This knowledge has in turn shaped and informed our thoughts about trauma and attachment.

Let's begin with the way that the brain develops. The brain builds outward from the primitive brain stem. The simplest functions, such as respiration and heart rate, are controlled deep within the brain. Moving outward and upward, the limbic and cortex areas control our emotions and complex thoughts. This simple-to-complex, bottom-to-top structure is the secret to the brain's capacity for survival. When an infant's brain develops, it happens sequentially, beginning with the bottom, regulatory regions, and moving up and out into more complex regions. The development of the brain is guided and influenced by experience. Neurons, or brain cells, change according to activities and experiences, building where they are activated, and creating learned knowledge and memories. Development is dependent on use. This dependence is essential to an understanding of the impact of neglect and trauma on children (Perry, n.d.).

During the first two to three years of life, neurons develop at a lightning pace. In fact, in these early years, they develop faster than at any other point in one's life. The brain is incredibly receptive to environment, and certain regions of the brain require specific experiences to develop. For example, while a baby possesses a sense of sight and all of the necessary visual "equipment" from day one, it takes six to eight months for the brain to develop the ability to fully process images, and a baby requires visual stimulation during that time period in order for the necessary neural pathways to grow.

 Much in the same way that systems such as our vision develop, so do our abilities to form emotional relationships. In the first years of life, we build neural pathways toward our ability to form relationships, to empathize, to care, and to love. Some of the first research to show the importance of those early years was conducted by Austro-Hungarian researcher Rene Spitz in the 1940s. Spitz (1946) followed two groups of children for several years, beginning at birth. The first group of children lived in a bare, clean orphanage. They were marooned in their cribs, receiving little focused attention, but their basic needs were consistently met by nurses. The second group of children was raised in a prison nursery. The children saw their mothers every day. They interacted with each other and the prison staff in a stimulating, if germy, environment. At four months old, the babies from both groups were developmentally interchangeable; however, at one year, those living in the orphanage lagged in motor skills, intellectual development, and physical health. Spitz had provided the first conclusive evidence of the essential nature of attachment.

 The ability to form relationships is the most fundamentally human part of us. This ability is essential to our ability to move through the world, to bond, to create families of our own, to work, and to survive. Neglect and other traumatic experiences may devastate neurodevelopment. When an infant is neglected or mistreated, the neural pathways that teach him how to love and connect—how to attach—fail to develop and thrive. His attempts to attach, to seek the responses in his caregivers that all babies seek—crying to indicate hunger, to be changed, to be held and comforted—are met intermittently or not at all. When these needs aren't met, the infant experiences high anxiety and terror. Neural systems are activated in response to fear, a survival system that, while essential in the moment, can over time create a persistent panic state, bathing the brain in the chemicals of fear and hyper-vigilance. Alternately, the infant may dissociate, retreating into a cold distance. These infants become children who may fail to bond with other people, who may lack trust and fear touch; ultimately, these children may be unable to attach and form the kinds of intimate and loving relationships that are so critical to a happy, healthy life.

Eric's inheritance was one of trauma and pain. He was born to heroin-addicted parents, and with a double hernia that wasn't identified or repaired until he was a toddler, meaning that the first two years of his life were marked by terrible pain. His mother left the home when he was only a year old. His father's addiction made his father inconsistent in his caregiving and his responses to his son. The multiple moves between placements that followed for Eric and his brother gave them both classic social histories for attachment disorder. Unlike his older brother Alex, however, Eric did not have the significant control issues that are associated with Reactive Attachment Disorder. However, Eric *was* hyper-vigilant, distrusting, emotionally distant, and reluctant to accept touch.

Knowing what we know now about trauma and the brain, it is possible to envision Eric's young brain, a poorly organized system, burdened with fear responses and overactive systems. Eric had been subjected to intense physical pain, neglect, abandonment—imagine every neural alarm sounding furiously. As a trainer, I often begin my discussions of attachment by drawing an outline of a child, my Eric, on a sheet of loose paper. "Here he is," I say, holding the paper Eric in front of me. "He is born to two drug-addicted parents"—I rip the paper in half. "He has a double hernia which no one has noticed or treated, and he lives in constant pain." I rip the two pieces I'm holding now in half. "When he was a year old, his mother left." I rip the pieces in half again. "He had surgery to repair his hernia." *Rip.* "He entered foster care." *Rip.* "He moved from foster home one, to two, to three, to four, to five." *Rip, rip, rip, rip, rip, rip.* I hold this handful of snowflakes, of confetti, out to the audience of caregivers, foster parents, and educators, imagining myself twenty years ago, faced with the challenge at hand. "Imagine that you are handed these pieces and told, 'Put these back together,'" I say. "What do you do?"

*What We Knew Then*

Today, I am able to look back through the lens of two decades of new knowledge on attachment, and understand more clearly the challenges we were facing with Eric and Alex. However, when they first entered our home I was working within the paradigms of the time. In the 1990s, the dominant model for a successful fostering practice was to create structure, and this was where we began with Eric and his older brother. The boys' previous foster home had minimal structure. The children in that home were expected to be home when the street lights turned on—something that wouldn't have been in option for us, regardless; in our home in the country, we didn't have street lights. Our home was a lot of fun, but we also had consistent expectations regarding school, activities, sports, and family trips. The rules were posted, but minimal:

1. Mom or Dad needs to know where you are at all times.
2. After school you eat a snack, do your homework, chore, and then play.
3. No electronics until after 6:00 p.m. on days when it is over 60 degrees and not raining.
4. No one is allowed in anyone else's room without a parent's permission.
5. Leave the toilet seat up when you are done.

The last rule was intended to be funny, but also to teach consideration of others. There were other rules that weren't posted, because they were indisputably part of our family culture. For example, hitting and violence were never allowed, and we ate meals as a family. The rules were adapted some over the years to meet the needs and structures that different children who came into our home required at the time.

There is not an exact formula for creating an environment that children respond to, but most children who entered our home did begin to thrive with consistent structure and clear expectations. Eric responded well to the structure and activities. His older brother

Alex, on the other hand, did not respond well to the environment in our home. He was exceptionally challenging for me; he was cruel to animals, inappropriately touched other children, and would complete chores in a way that made things remarkably worse. He also knew how to triangulate my husband Jim and me; his disrespect for me in tandem with his warmth toward Jim made me—and others—question my sanity. When Alex and Eric came into our home, we were told it would be just a short placement – at the most six months. They were visiting their father and working toward reunification in that relationship, but their father was a heroin addict. Six months turned into a year, and a year into two. After two years in our home, Alex was becomingly more and more difficult to supervise. Increasingly, I feared for the safety of the other children due to his size; he was now six foot and three hundred pounds, with an escalating disregard of boundaries. After a year of failed attempts to find placements which would take him, he was placed at a local residential facility. He stayed at the facility until he completed high school.

When Alex left our home, I felt a rush of conflicting emotions. I was incredibly relieved, while Jim was sad; he and I had not experienced the same child. I felt guilty. I had failed this child, and I had separated him from his brother. However, in the larger picture, our experience with Alex was important. I began to research some of his behaviors, and I began to understand that he had significant attachment issues. Eric's attachment issues, while clearly present, were not coupled with Alex's intense anger. In the darkness of having to send Alex to a new placement, I focused on leveraging my new knowledge of attachment toward Eric's healing.

*Permanency, Constancy, and the Chameleon Effect*

As we dive deeper into our discussion of attachment, I want to explain the connection between attachment and identity formation. Let's begin with object relations, a psychoanalytic psychology theory. The premise of the theory is that a child's identity is a reflection of the mother-infant dyad. The mother-infant experience is responsible for the formation of a child's identity during the first three years of his life. Object relations theory holds that a person's mind develops as a direct result of these primary relationships. The "objects" represent perceptions of real people in a person's life experience. Because these relationships are forged in infancy, they continue to pervade a person's existence throughout his life. In Holly van Gulden and Ann Sutton's (2014) book, *And You Are Still You*, the authors state:

> Object relations theory hypothesizes that people develop their sense of themselves in the world, through their experiences (and their perceptions of those experiences) with their primary caregivers. The object or caregiver is the gatekeeper through which the infant/child experiences the world, and therefore, herself in the world. The infant's relationship with the world, as experienced through her interactions with the caregivers, begins with the physical exploration of the external world (outside the womb) and culminates in the formation of an internal structure of self (p. 42).

Through object relationships in infancy, we gain two essential things: permanency and constancy. According to van Gulden & Sutton (2014), permanency is the capacity to trust and take for granted that objects, important people, and the self will continue to exist, even when they are out of an individual's sensory contact. Constancy, on the other hand, is the sensory experience of unconditional love. A sense of constancy begins to develop at the age of three, when the child starts to understand that the angry parent and the loving, nurturing parent are one and the same, and doing something wrong does not negate the parent's love. Permanency and constancy are the building blocks and stability of the ego. They offer self-resilience and the ability to change, adapt, and transition. They are critical for emotional health, for a child to know that the caregiver and the beliefs that the caregiver holds about the child will continue to exist across time, space, emotion, and experience. If the child perceives himself as valuable because his primary caregiver perceives him as valuable, the child will reject negative messages that tell him he is bad or worthless when he is confronted with them.

In a healthy attachment relationship, it is by the fourth or fifth week of life that the infant has developed the trust cycle with his primary caregiver. The attachment made between the infant and caregiver is a sensory connection. During the wonderful attachment cycle, the parent meets the infant's needs and the infant experiences the caregiver through his senses, including the sixth sense, the proprioception sense. This is the sense of body position in space and the sense of movement. No two caregivers affect the child in the same way, and changes in caregivers can cause an infant to feel unsafe. This insecurity has significant implications, I believe, for child welfare practice as well as infant adoption, where in some cases the infant goes into a temporary foster home before the adoptive family. By the time the infant is in the adoptive home, the adoptive parent is the third caregiver for the infant to adjust to—or to not adjust to, as the case may be.

The second stage of this relational development is differentiation, when the child's sense of oneness with the primary caregiver evolves into a sense of separateness with a secure connection to the caregiver. During this time the child begins to learn to self-soothe, often using a transitional object. The process involves the child coming to know that the caregiver continues to exist when the caregiver is away from him. The child also comes to know that the beliefs and perception the caregiver has about him remain intact, even from a distance. In other words, the child begins to develop permanency and constancy, believing that the caregiver is permanent even when out of sight. The infant or child begins to integrate the belief in the caregiver's permanent existence with his own permanency and security.

As the child develops permanency and constancy, the need for the transitional object is reduced. This is a conflictive stage; the child desires independence while also wanting closeness. As the child experiences increased success in his independence, the success reinforces the positive feelings of self that were set in place by the primary caregiver.

Permanency and constancy are remarkably damaged in children who have experienced trauma. Children who have not experienced a warm, nurturing home environment only see what is presented to them. They believe people may disappear. They believe that anger from a caregiver means the caregiver no longer loves them. Children who experience multiple, inconsistent, or abusive caregivers during their first three years have no sense of who they are; they become who they are with. They do not have an integrated sense of self, and so will present different parts of themselves to different people. These are the children who, once they are no longer under their adoptive parents' close, external limits, make choices that are incredibly contrary to "the way that they were raised." The children may have complied, to some degree, while in the homes of their foster/adoptive parents. But once out of the home, these young adults begin to make choices very contrary to the values they learned at home. These children become chameleons.

Earlier in this chapter, I spoke of how Jim and I experienced Alex as two different people. Many foster and adoptive parents share that pain—a child presents as a solid, Christian young person with a sincere heart, who regularly attends church and youth group; however, around certain peers, the child is suddenly abusing drugs and exhibiting sexually promiscuous behaviors. How can a child or adolescent seemingly be two people? How should a parent respond to a child who seems to be a chameleon, becoming the crowd he is with? I had the opportunity to hear Holly van Gulden, an attachment therapist and adoptive parent whose book I referenced above, speak at a foster parent conference, where she shared the story of her adoptive son. She stated that when he left home, "He didn't take me with him!" I thought about this idea for a long time—in fact, it took me some years to begin to understand what she meant. However, as I experienced chameleon-like adolescents and adults, I began to see that they had very minimal self-identities. Children and adolescents came into my home with very little sense of who they were.

Through Holly van Gulden's speech about her son, I realized that one of the most important elements of my work with children is helping them to receive and internalize my message of who they are. A positive, healthy attachment relationship with a primary caregiver helps children to learn this, experience this, and internalize this sense of self. In my own life, this attachment relationship was with my mother. She put me to bed each night and told me I was pretty, I was smart, and I was capable of doing anything I wanted to with my life. I carry her image of me as part of who I am. Children coming from neglectful families often carry negative messages, or none at all. My role as a foster/adoptive parent was to develop that message and give it to the child to carry with them, even when I am far from them. As a therapist, I work with people to develop that message, often through how I see them, so they can carry the message with them. For those with a faith base, I work with them on carrying the message of how God sees them.

In practice, how do we leverage our attachment relationships to create that message and facilitate permanency and constancy in children who did not receive that message in the first three years? The premise of healing trauma is to provide a child with an environment of safety. We believe that if we remove the stressors of an abusive environment and provide safety, the child will heal. But the child has to perceive that he is safe; he can't just be told that he is safe. Creating a true sense of safety for a child requires us to consider what didn't happen developmentally for the child in his first three years of life, and work to recreate those developmental stages in the child, regardless of what chronological age he may be. This recreation begins with the symbiotic dance of caregiver and child, which allows the child to integrate the caregiver's unconditional love and value into his sense of self. The caregiver is the mirror of the child and the reflection of the world for the child. This mirror and reflection are experienced by the child through his interactions with the primary caregiver. The stability of the relationship between child and caregiver becomes the foundation of the child's internal sense of self.

Van Gulden and Sutton (2014) equate this process to the experience of falling in love:

> The dance of attachment between a parent and new child, who is not an infant, or between two adults develops from the fog of two separate "individuals" meeting and learning each other's cues, to the often tantalizing and simultaneously frightening merging of lives to form a unit. This step is maintaining the

connection without losing either the relationship or the separate 'identities' (p. 15).

That first "fog" stage van Gulden and Sutton (2014) describe is the stage everyone in a new attachment or relationship experiences. In a caregiver/child relationship, it is the caregiver's responsibility to interpret the child's needs and meet those needs both physically and psychologically. This work includes assisting the child to manage his distress, meet his needs, and assist him to a state of calmness, just as the attachment cycle occurs with an infant. In this process with the child, as in the attachment cycle with an infant, trust is built.

Positive interactions have to be intentional to recreate this attachment. The attachment should not be dependent on the child's performance or behavior, but on the relationship. The message of "I enjoy you" is given to the infant or child, and the infant or child sends back the signal of "I enjoy us" to the primary caregiver. The infant or child experiences himself as one with the primary caregiver, and the caregiver provides positive feedback to the infant or child just for *being*. These positive interactions are simple – a simple eye gazing of joy at the infant or child, a touch, a wink, or a smile that communicates love. These are interactions that can be done with every infant or child. The critical piece of internalizing a sense of self is created when the child internalizes the messages *I am worthwhile; I am valuable; I am loved; I am capable; I can give and receive joy.*

Through continuing positive interactions and through intentional eye contact and close personal connections, trust as well as the child's sense of his own positive value continue to develop. These developments occur just as they do in the attachment cycle with an infant. This attachment dance moves the relationship with the child from the stage of fog to one of identity with the primary caregiver. As this child is increasingly connected to the caregiver, feeling safe, protected, nurtured and valued by the caregiver, the child begins to accept and internalize the message of his or her value.

For toddlers, as independence becomes the norm, a stage called rapprochement occurs, and will occur similarly in recreated attachment. The child exhibits distress when separated from the caregiver, and attempts to return to the safety and security of the earlier oneness with the caregiver. As the caregiver reassures and nurtures the child, the caregiver also needs to promote the child's independence through support and by emotionally refueling the child. Van Gulden and Sutton (2014) state,

> "If the toddler is not encouraged to return to independent exploration she may never experience separateness as safe, may never solidify permanence: the capacity to know that the parent still exists and keeps her safe, even when she is out of touch or focus" (p. 25).

Often it is difficult to experience the child at his developmental level, rather than his chronological age level—to remember that an older child may be much younger developmentally. However, it is imperative to return the child, no matter his age, to his developmental level, often starting with the earliest experiential needs of the child through the attachment cycle. As these earliest relational needs are met, the child begins to view himself through the loving, accepting eyes of the primary caregiver. The child begins to internalize this message and view himself as valuable, loveable, and worthwhile.

Van Gulden and Sutton (2014) suggest that for children with no constancy in their lives, caregivers should provide discipline in a manner similar to how they would approach a three-year-old. The authors advocate for a firm reprimand in a serious tone, but with calm and non-threatening body language. Then, after repetition, the caregiver should immediately provide a positive sensory experience to the child, such as a hug or an affirmation. This positive interaction helps the child to see that while his caregiver is unhappy with the behavior, the child is still loved and loveable.

Helping people to understand their own strengths and talents as well as their struggles is essential to assisting them to develop a true sense of who they uniquely are. I learned the importance of teaching children that they are intrinsically valuable later in my experience as a parent and professional. My son Allen has kept himself somewhat removed from our family. This past year he has, however, connected more frequently with us. He flew to Florida this past Christmas to join us for a few days. The last night, he and I were alone, the only ones still awake. I said to him, "I think I haven't told you how proud I am of you."

He replied, very shocked, asking, "Why would you be proud of me?" His response saddened me. He had not internalized my view of him as a loveable, valuable member of our family. As I responded, talking about his achievements, I realized I was giving him a very performance-based response, as though his value came only from his successes. I realized he needs to hear that he is worthwhile, loveable, and valued by me because he is my son. I know that, even though he is 29, I still have work to do on his understanding of my value of him and his sense of self. For those of us who have been given the gift of being the unconditional caregivers for rejected and cast off children of all ages, that work is our job.

*Facilitating Attachment through the Senses*

As we discussed above, attachment occurs through the senses, beginning with the touch, sight, sustenance, and comfort that the caregiver provides. All of this sensory input builds attachment. As I began to focus more on facilitating attachment, I began to consider how our children interacted with our home environment, and how I might use my knowledge of the senses to increase attachment with Eric and the other children in our home. I think that these sensory techniques can work on a daily basis to help create attachment between caregivers and children.

Smell and taste are related, and food smells are some of our deepest memories. I cooked bacon and cinnamon rolls on the weekends at our house, to create a smell memory and to build attachment in these moments through food. Food is a means of acknowledging that you are thinking about a child, that you want to do something special for him. Historically, food has been a means of connection. The symbolism of breaking bread is not arbitrary, and while food has its own set of complications, it also has a lot of leverage in the world of attachment. When our family took in new children, we would often visit McDonald's on the first night, because of its familiarity; the food is the same everywhere. Beyond that first night, I often show a child that I care about him by preparing something he alone likes. "Obtaining" might be a more accurate word—no one is completely adept at creating all of the hallmarks of a child's home culture. One of our teenagers, DeShawn, wanted chitlins for Thanksgiving, and I knew what that would mean to him—an affirmation of his identity, a sense that he could preserve his home culture in his new surroundings. However, cooking pig intestines on Thanksgiving morning was not something I was versed in, or even ready to try. However, there was a woman at our church who made and sold chitlins, and we were able to get some from her—a small gesture that meant a lot to DeShawn. Most gestures like this do mean a lot—they show the child that you see him. Another technique I used was to lock up the snack foods. Putting a lock on the snack cabinet managed hoarding, but it also meant that when the children wanted a nurturing, high carbohydrate food, such as a granola bar, they would need to come to me. There were endless healthier snacks but the snack food was more limited; I used those attachment-forming sweets as a means of connection.

Research shows that lavender and lemon are two key scents for building attachment, so I began to bring these scents into the house in easy ways—candles, for example. Today, when my granddaughter comes to visit for the weekends, one of the first attachment-building things we do is to put on lavender lotion together.

Visually, scholar and practitioner Julie Alvarado promotes the concept of emotional regulation through color and visual design. The most calming environment for a traumatized child is a room with nothing hanging from the ceiling; we tend to think of mobiles as synonymous with infants, but a traumatized child will do better in a room with a blank ceiling. Alvarado argues for blank walls and for lamps, and for creating an environment of order. I tried to create order in our home and to avoid a lot of clutter; clutter was directly related to tension in our home. Messiness was confined to bedrooms, where you could close the door.

Aurally, many foster homes use calming music. In our home, we worked to build the environment for hearing, in contrast to homes where the television plays constantly. Noise is often exponential; people talk over each other and the television is turned up, and so on. In our home, the layout of the house allowed us to make the basement into a family room, confining the television noise to the downstairs.

Touch, of course, is perhaps the greatest key to attachment. Some of the things I would learn about attachment as I began my research were things that we had already observed through experience. The idea of recreating the developmental stages that children have missed has also been referred to as "meeting children where they are." The beginning of this knowledge manifested in the holding therapies of the eighties, where children were held and rocked by therapists, or endured other practices intended to "return them" to infancy. However, many of the initial approaches pushed in the eighties had the potential to cause more fear in a child—a child who is held by force, for instance, will experience only fear, not attachment. It is true that children with attachment issues tend to seek out attachment at the level they need to begin growing their neural pathways; they essentially return to the site where they left off. I saw this clearly when an eleven-year-old girl we fostered would climb into my lap while I was feeding my infant son; she was seeking out experiences of attachment from the time period where they had been interrupted, beginning the process of completing her poorly developed neurological systems of attachment as I rocked her.

By the time I was working with Eric, I had learned through experience that children will point you toward the attachments they need; it is your job to intuit those behaviors from the cues that children provide you with, to provide safe opportunities for attachment, touch, and intimacy, but not to force them. When he came into our home, Eric wouldn't accept touch, though I ached to provide him with physical comfort. Even when he was very sick, he wouldn't let me touch him; in those times, when Alex was still with us, I asked Alex to sit with Eric. Alex's arm around him was the smallest comfort that Eric would accept.

I remember the first time that Eric let me touch him. He had been with us for a year and a half, and I put my hand on his while we prayed. Over time, he would let me regularly touch his hands when we prayed at night. We were making progress that I could see and feel, as real as the warmth of his hand under my own.

*Attachment Beyond Infancy*

As Eric grew older, Jim and I were faced with the challenge of continuing to intentionally facilitate attachment during a time in his life when his job, developmentally, was to pull away. Attempting to coddle an older child who is asserting his independence is going to have an opposite effect from the one you're looking for. Attachment occurs during times of high emotion. A baby cries, and the caregiver meets the baby's needs and calms the baby down. Replicating that attachment cycle beyond infancy is an exercise in great intention.

Eric had likely been exposed to alcohol in utero, and he had some of the characteristics of Fetal Alcohol Syndrome, or FAS. He had a lazy eye, so we spent many hours going to a specialized eye doctor and doing exercises, none of which worked. He had to wear a patch at times to try to strengthen the muscle. Later, when we adopted Eric, he was covered by our insurance and had corrective surgery. However, the long hours that we spent together doing eye exercises in those early years were a great opportunity to be close and make eye contact, tedious though it often seemed.

The physical touch I worked toward with Eric as he grew older was careful; I seized opportunities for physical touch that would have been rejected if I had been more overt. I would rub his shoulders as he played Starcraft computer games with his brothers. On trips we would be forced to be close for long periods of time, shoulder to shoulder; in a movie theatre I would make sure I was sitting next to the child who needed touch the most. For a child who has not been touched, who has not formed those attachments, sitting shoulder-to-shoulder is a small nick in that armor.

When Eric was about nine, he, Jim, and our son Ivan enrolled in a wrestling club. As Eric moved into junior high, it became apparent that he was a good wrestler. Sports can be incredibly therapeutic for children who have experienced trauma. They give children an excellent physical outlet for anger; they develop cause-and-effect thinking; they encourage children to work with others and promote leadership skills; and they create motivation for maintaining good grades and behavior. Sports are also an important opportunity for fostering attachment, because these are times of high emotion. I sat through a lot of really awful (for me) wrestling meets for those moments of high emotion, when Eric would be so excited that he would forget that he didn't want to hug me. It gave him and Jim a way to connect physically, as well; they would wrestle together, practicing moves and, without realizing it, meeting some of Eric's needs for physical contact, the kind of "skin hunger" that Perry and Szalavitz (2006) describe in children who have grown up never being fed essential loving touch.

Humor was another essential means of forming attachment in our home as our children grew older. Within the working model of attachment, children experience the world as a place that can't be trusted, and in order to change this, new neural pathways must be created. Scholar-practitioner Karen Purvis states that it takes one hundred new repetitions of an experience in order to create a new neural pathway; however, if there is humor involved, that number of repetitions drops to twelve. This staggering difference is due to chemical that is released in the brain when people are laughing. We laughed a lot in our household.

I also learned of the technique of introducing the boys as "my boys." Generally, no one knew Eric was not our biological child. I had pictures of all the boys up around the house. I also made sure that Eric knew the importance of his role in our family; I referred to him as the "spark" of our family, and indeed, when he was at his grandparents' house for the weekend, it felt like our family was very quiet.

*Jim's Approach: Shoulder-to-Shoulder Attachment*

In discussing attachment beyond infancy, I want to especially acknowledge the impact Jim, my husband, had on the children we fostered. This book is written in a singular first person point of view from my perspective for the ease of telling our story. The point of view perhaps gives an unbalanced view of our partnership and our work. We have built our life and family together, and even in the writing of this book he has been instrumental and without fail by my side. One of our great strengths as parents has been in our different approaches. In building attachment, for instance, Jim was much more focused building attachment through shared experiences.

    Jim's approach to attachment was much more about doing things with the boys together, shoulder to shoulder, from home improvement activities to basic car repair. He taught most of the young men in our home how to change oil, rotate tires, change brake pads, put up dry wall, and, even for a few, wire electricity. He redid a room in our house because he felt that the group of young men in our house should learn the processes behind the remodeling. Jim was also brought a lot of fun into our home by camping, biking, canoeing, and caving with many of the boys. These adventures were often the hardest, but most rewarding, experiences that many of these young men had ever experienced. The times they spent in the wilderness, away from home, and working together, were often very novel but rewarding experiences for the boys.

    Some of the young men did not respond to his approach; some had no interest in work projects, car repair, or outdoor adventures. Jim still tried to engage these young men in learning skills, but some were resistive, and this created friction. If they did not want to participate, Jim would not force them, but would instead try to create fun even in the midst of work projects, making the work enticing even for those who were less enthusiastic. It was sad for me that some of these young men missed the opportunity to learn key skills that would help them throughout their lives. Those who were willing to learn from Jim still speak of the value of those experiences.

    Jim's approach to teaching a strong work ethic while having fun was very impactful for many of our teen boys, but it especially influenced our youngest son, Louis. Because of Louis's past experiences with foster/adoptive mothers who rejected him, he was very reticent and wary of trusting me. But Jim was very experiential in his approach with Louis; they worked on many projects and activities together. Initially, Louis wouldn't complete the projects well, but Jim's approach was to be accepting even if the work was poor. Jim would work with Louis until things were done correctly, but in a noncritical way. Louis was accepting of Jim's approach, and connected with him strongly. He is now a young man who is hired to do odd jobs while he is in college, and recommended to others because of the excellence of the work he does. He continues to be very connected to Jim, who, other than his wife, is the person Louis feels the safest with. Jim is a person who is very consistent, and that consistency along with his shoulder-to-shoulder presence have worked to make many young men feel safe and to build attachment in a way that was invaluable in our family.

*Looking Forward, Looking Back*

As Eric grew older, he became more gifted academically. In high school, he took higher level courses and graduated 17th in his class. He received both academic and wrestling scholarships to Bethel College. He attended Bethel for two years, but their wrestling program was discontinued, and Eric opted to join the army. Being in Special Forces as a Green Beret was his dream from the time he was a little boy; I believe he uses some of what others might see as the effects of his early childhood as strengths—his hyper-vigilance, emotional detachment, and obsession with physical fitness. He has also completed his bachelor's degree through the military.

One goal I had for Eric was to become attached enough to me to be able to attach to a lifelong partner. After Eric completed his Special Forces Qualification Course, he moved to Clarksville. He came home for a visit in the summer and decided he wanted to find a partner. As with everything else he does, he was very determined and by Christmas, at a holiday rental condo in Gulf Shores, Alabama, our whole family was introduced to Michelle. Michelle was the first girl I had to share my boys with, and I did it very willingly. She came into our family seeming to love all the boys instantly, instinctively knowing how to make each of them feel special. She played board game after board game—frequently winning—and our family fell in love with her, too. True again to Eric's way of doing things, when he sets his mind on something, he does it. He came home from his first deployment to Iraq on a Tuesday and they were married on Friday; we quickly went down to Tennessee for their wedding. They had a more formal ceremony in October. I am very thankful for Michelle and her steady influence on Eric. She is a beautiful, brilliant woman who is completely accepting of our huge, unique family. She is also an amazing mother to my grandson, "Little Eric." It is very fulfilling to see Eric have such ability to love and care for both of them.

Eric still seems physically distant at times, but he is often the first to respond to texts and emails and is very good at calling me on a regular basis; I know he is deeply committed both to his and our families. Perry and Szalavitz (2006) talk about "loving with an accent," the sense that attachment and love are not first languages for children who have experienced trauma and neglect. Still, I think of how I always ended those trainings, when I stood holding an avalanche of paper scraps in my hands, the pieces of my child who had experienced so much before the age of six. I began to tape the pieces together, slowly. I pieced them together with intention, working with precision and patience. When I was finished, I held up the paper to the audience—the rough figure of my son. Where the tape had bonded the pieces together, those fractures had grown stronger. It wasn't possible to tear the paper any more. He was, though changed, stronger, and once again whole.

# CHAPTER TWO

## THE KNIFE IN THE KITCHEN: BEING AWARE OF THE SOURCE OF THE TRAUMA

## The Knife in the Kitchen: Being Aware of the Source of Trauma

In 1989, we moved three hours to the east. We were still therapeutic foster parents at that time, working with a community mental health center in our area. The first child placed in our new home was a ten-year-old girl named Angela. As is the case with many foster children, we didn't have comprehensive information about Angela's history. We knew that her last foster home had been deemed too punitive; when Angela misbehaved, she was punished by being made to run laps around the house or to complete relentless sets of jumping jacks. She had been removed from her birth mother because of her mother's prostitution, and there was speculation that Angela herself may have been involved.

Angela lived with us during the time I was pregnant and gave birth to Alex, my youngest biological child. She was cooperative, and she seemed to feel safe in our home. We involved her in community activities, such as gymnastics and the church youth group. She had visits with her mother in our home, and then her mother began to pick her up for unsupervised visits. I struggled watching the men who often accompanied Angela's mother; I had little background information, so I could only speculate about her past, a heavy feeling in my stomach.

One spring afternoon, Angela was sitting at the kitchen table doing her homework while I stood at the kitchen sink, peeling potatoes. "I don't get how to do this," she complained, and I turned around, the paring knife in my hand.

In seconds, Angela was under the table, screaming. I put the knife down and crawled under the table to hold her. "I'm not going to hurt you," I kept saying, over and over again. "I know that it must have been scary to see the knife. I'm not going to hurt you."

Regardless of how much or how little information is provided for the foster or adoptive parent about the past history of the child, there will always be trauma and experiences that may be triggered in the child without warning. So much of working with traumatized children is doing good detective work, and responding to behavior with the knowledge that the child's response is due to trauma. That spring afternoon, I sat in the dark, close space beneath the table, holding this little girl in my arms. I couldn't have known until that moment that a paring knife would offer me a clue to the violence she had witnessed and endured. What I could do was respond to it as a manifestation of those experiences, let that information inform my future parenting, and keep working to understand the trauma mapped on her small brain and body.

*The Traumatized Brain*

The dominant view of trauma during the time we had Angela, and during the years that followed, held that children are resilient. In Bruce Perry's and Maia Szalavitz's *The Boy Who was Raised as a Dog* (2006), Perry describes being walked through a murder scene by a colleague, and seeing three children, dotted in blood and saucer-eyed, who had witnessed their parents' murder. "What about the children?" Perry asks, and the colleague responds dismissively, "Children are resilient. They will be fine" (p. 38).

The reality is that children are in a particularly vulnerable position to have their brains literally shaped by trauma. But how does this happen, and why? To explain how childhood trauma manifests itself through behavior years later, we need to turn again to the exquisitely sensitive brain.

Dr. Bessel A. Van der Kolk, a researcher at Boston University who has worked extensively in the field of trauma since the 1970s, produced one of the first integrative texts, *Psychological Trauma* (2003), on the impact of trauma on individuals. He has also done extensive research on the fear response, utilizing Magnetic Resonance Imaging (MRI) to provide us with images of how the brain reacts in response to fear. When a threat is perceived, the amygdala activates quickly. It works in conjunction with the hippocampus to release hormones, including cortisol, and activates many additional body systems in order to prepare for protection. We refer to these responses as the fight, flight, or freeze response: For fight or flight, increased blood flow to the muscles begins; blood pressure elevates for extra energy; muscle tension increases for extra strength; and the blood clotting function speeds up, in case of injury. The stories we hear of sudden intense strength—the mother who is able to lift a car off of a child;

the weekend hiker who is suddenly able to scale a tree to escape a cougar—come from this amygdala-triggered physical ability. Alternately, the freeze response may set off a different set of systems, the response that the brain triggers when it seems like there is no hope. This is sometimes thought of as the "playing dead" response. The blood pressure drops to conserve lost blood, and the individual "plays dead," which can often be a lifesaving move.

Evolutionarily, the fear response served a concrete and very necessary purpose. If you are a hunter–gatherer being chased by an animal, it's very important that in a crucial moment you have the increased blood flow and respiratory capacity—or alternately, the ability to play dead—in order to get away or to survive an attack. However, in our modern lives, it is also essential to have a brain function that determines whether a threat is real or imagined. This is the role of the frontal lobes. As the brain grows out and up, the frontal lobes are an area that develops later, and governs higher functions: right and wrong, cause and effect, the ability to resist impulses, the ability to plan ahead, and the ability to decide if a threat needs to be acted upon by the body.

The classic example of the function of the frontal lobes is that of Phineas Gage, a railroad foreman who lived in Vermont in the late 19th century. Well-liked and handsome, Gage was twenty-five on the autumn day when he was using a tamping iron to pack explosives. The explosives detonated, and the iron—thirteen pounds and over three feet long—pierced his cheek and exited through his skull, leaving him blind in one eye but, shockingly, alive. Gage's survival alone was remarkable, but it was what happened after the accident that secured Gage a place in the hall of neurological fame: Gage was a different man. He was an animal, his friends claimed; he was profane and uncaring; he no longer seemed to possess a high intellect; he lied and stole. The railroad company fired him, and he went on to drive coaches. He died at 36 after suffering several seizures. The shift in his personality eventually provided the first documented link between trauma and personality change; his skull, preserved now at Harvard University, shows how the rod had penetrated a section of his prefrontal cortex (Twomey, 2010).

It's easy to imagine that after his accident, Phineas Gage might not have reacted well to perceived threats. His compromised frontal lobes would have lacked the higher level connections necessary to distinguish between real threats and perceived ones. A more intact or developed frontal lobe will be able to recognize a false threat and send a message to the amygdala, reducing the fear response. However, in children who have been chronically or complexly traumatized, the cortex has been flooded with cortisol. In the same way that Gage's impaired cortex would not have been likely to detect a real versus an imagined threat, a cortisol-flooded cortex will be ineffective at sorting out threats, and the "threat" will be met with extreme responses—emotional outbursts, inward suffering, or dissociation. Dr. Van der Kolk (2002) explains the traumatized frontal cortex as a prisoner, "held hostage by a volatile amygdala. Thinking is hijacked by emotion. [Traumatized people] are very sensitively tuned to respond to even very minor stimuli as if their life is in danger."

The fear experienced under constant threat actually reshapes the brain, shutting down its higher regions. The abilities to create, to plan, and to think critically are not useful in a fight, flight, or freeze situation. However, under constant duress, those areas of the brain become constantly compromised, reshaping a brain with little frontal cortex development. In the short-term, the fight, flight, or freeze adaption makes sense, and can be life-saving. However, in the long run, it can diminish an individual's ability to progress in areas of intellect, reasoning, critical thinking, and reflection. In their book *Born for Love: Why Empathy is Essential—and Endangered*, Perry and Szalavitz (2010) suggest that this kind of reshaping may explain some of the darker periods of human history. The authors point to the Dark Ages, when human experiences were marked with great fear, warfare, little art, and short, brutal life spans; "Because just as children grow up as a reflection of the developmental environment provided by their parents and immediate family, so does the inventiveness, creativity, and productivity of a people reflect the development environment of their society" (Szalavitz & Perry, 2010, p. 117).

Unfortunately, the reshaping of the brain is not confined to childhood, but may begin even before birth. Robin Karr-Morse and Meredith Wiley (1997) suggest that prenatal drug, nicotine, and alcohol exposure, as well as other prenatal stressors such as domestic violence, may bring a child into the world with an already overly active nervous system. The amygdala is completely formed by six months prenatally; with prenatal trauma exposure and physical and emotional neglect in early infancy, a child's brain may be wired for violent behavior and impulsivity before he's seen a birthday. Infants show different symptoms than adults as a result of this early onset trauma. According to Levine & Kline (2007), "This is due to a combination of factors including brain development, level of reasoning and perceptual development, incomplete personality formation and dependency, as well as attachment to their caregivers. Together with restricted motor and language skills, children have limited capacities to respond or cope."

    Neither does the shaping of the brain cease after early childhood. Dr. Jay Giedd, a neuroscientist at the National Institute of Health, has used brain scans to identify consistent, continued growth in the teen cerebral cortex, including the parietal and temporal lobes; these are the areas of the brain associated with logic, spatial reasoning, and language. However, his most noteworthy finding was the complex, ongoing growth in the frontal lobes—the areas of the brain associated with executive functioning, impulse control, right and wrong, and planning. Giedd determined that the peak growth is at eleven years for girls, and twelve for boys; growth continues, however, past the age of twenty. Post-pubescent growth is specialized, meaning that the areas that are exercised continue to develop in a use-it-or-lose-it process of pruning. This means that teens' positive and negative experiences affect their "final" brains. Another study demonstrated that teens often respond to fear through their amygdalas, because their frontal cortexes are not yet fully developed. Emotions for the teens measured became less distinct; for instance, teens were likely to confuse fear and anger. These findings can explain the emotional overreactions which are classically associated with the teen years; stimuli are being processed in the emotional area of the brain, rather than in an area for higher thought and processing (Straugh, 2003).

In other words, the brain is continually being shaped according to our period of development and our experiences. It is a highly complex system of input and output, a constantly evolving sponge.

*The Shape of Trauma*

"That happened so long ago"; "He's been in my home for years"; "She should be over that by now." Often, we think of trauma as having a distinct timeline, a statute of limitations on when we must expect to see its manifestations. However, the body does not forget trauma, even when the event is no longer consciously remembered. I have often heard it stated that the trauma is in the child's cells.

Additionally, when we experience trauma, the ever-developing brain can create connections between otherwise separate things: a paring knife carries the emotional memory of violence. The scent of Acqua di Parma becomes inexorably linked to the fear of the abusive father who wore it. The ash color of a shirt is the same shade as the paint on the wall in the home where so much abuse took place. Our memories are not distinct, and they inform our current experiences and behaviors. Our associations gather weight; they snowball; they continue to assert their influence long after the specific experiences have past. When one of the five senses signals a threat, the signal of fear initiates the fight, flight, or freeze response. The body often responds as if the original threat is occurring (Levine & Kline, 2007).

Imagine Angela's young brain, in our kitchen, over twenty years ago. The trauma she had endured meant her brain had developed to be on constant high alert; the reptilian brain stem housing the flight, flight, or freeze response was overdeveloped. When I turned with the paring knife in my hand, the sudden flash of metal through the air registered as the original threat, and the amygdala sent a message to the brain stem to respond. Her frontal cortex, awash in cortisol, lacked the ability to distinguish between the original threat and the harmless potato peeling that I was doing at the sink.

A child's response is automatic, rather than thought out or

reasoned. The wiring of a traumatized child's brain means that many experiences are perceived as threatening, even when they aren't. Parents, caregivers, and professionals will often ask a child, "Why did you do that?" or "What happened?" This kind of question is impossible for the child to answer; the experience was processed through the reptilian brain stem, leaving the child little memory or ability to understand and decipher the situation. Additionally, the brain will continue to flood with cortisol; while this is an attempt to calm the brain, it continues to limit the child's capacity for thinking and reasoning.

As providers, caregivers, foster parents/adoptive parents, we often see the behavioral manifestations of trauma. We see these children raging, easily triggered into strong reactions, showing poor impulse control and a lack of cause and effect thinking; we see them distracted and shutting down. We see them growing over-stimulated, spinning like out-of-control tops. These children can go from zero to sixty in seconds, becoming hyper-aroused, their amygdalas flooded with chemicals, even with very little visible provocation. Alternately, some children internalize their trauma, dissociating, self-harming, and withdrawing from relationships. The response to trauma is often compartmentalized; the mind and body seem to separate in order to avoid an overwhelming rush of memories of trauma. While this reaction is involuntary, it can be seen by others as distraction, inattentiveness, and daydreaming. Somatic complaints plague many traumatized children, as do sleep struggles. There is evidence that shows that how a child responds may be in part determined by gender; boys tend to externalize their symptoms, while girls tend toward the internal (Levine & Kline, 2007).

The manifestations of trauma for teens are also profound. Teens who have witnessed violence are more likely to abuse substances; those who have experienced physical abuse are twice as likely to suffer from depression; those who have experienced sexual assault are dramatically more likely to be diagnosed with PTSD. Substance abuse, danger-seeking activities, and early or reckless sexual activity are all ways that trauma manifests; however, this behavior often looks oppositional and defiant, causing problems in school, relationships, and the family (Levine & Kline, 2007). Sexual abuse at any age impacts the core of a child's developing sense of self; it involves significant shame and guilt, and distortions of one's understanding and experience of self. The child or teen, rather than perceiving the abuse as bad, perceives him or herself as bad. Many individuals experience dissociation as a way to emotionally manage these horrific experiences. As we've discussed, this can manifest itself in forgetfulness, distractions, learning difficulties, and trouble forming close, intimate relationships.

*Using What We Know*

A traumatized child is incapable of recognizing the source of his distress. The child will act out his trauma through behaviors, and he is dependent on their caregivers to determine the sources of distress that result in his behaviors. The responsibility of the caregiver is to meet the needs of the child, to regulate the child, and to create an environment of safety, security, and nurturance. This environment of safety and security is key to the child's healing process.

Often when a child responds in a way we, as caregivers and professionals, see as inappropriate, our reaction is to respond with stronger and greater intensity. This reaction only continues the onslaught of trauma on the brain. The flood of cortisol escalates the behavior, and in the long-term results in a brain shaped by fear. Our first response as caregivers has to be one of calmness, mirroring self-regulation, rather than meeting the child's behavior with our own fear response. One foster mother I worked with related the experience of walking in on her two foster children in their bedroom, and finding one child lying on top of the other. Knowing the importance of self-regulation, she closed the door, took several deep breaths, and then reentered the room. She knew that if she reacted from her initial response, it would increase the trauma of the children, and instead she responded to the situation calmly, minimizing the children's fright, shame, and embarrassment. This kind of spectacular response stops the vicious cycle of fear response and the flood of cortisol that can be so damaging to children raised in environments of fear and reaction.

For those children who respond through what are often called "rages," the best response again is to remain calm. It is important to assure the child that the adult is in charge and will keep the child safe. The adult should use a tone of voice which conveys an understanding of the intensity of the child's feelings, and at the same times assures protection and hope. It is essential that the adult remains with the child, providing an experience of safety and consistent protection. During this experience for the child, the adult is providing reassurance, rather than rejection and condemnation. This response promotes the relationship and attachment with the child. Many times caregivers will use a "time-out" strategy, or send a child to his or her room to calm down. A more effective and nurturing strategy is to use a "time-in"—instead of banishing the child, the adult should remain with the child until he or she is calm. Doing so provides a powerful message to the child of safety and protection, as well as a sense that the adult's love for the child is not conditional on his or her behavior.

Clare was the first child we had who expressed her trauma experiences through rages. She was seven when she came into our home with her little sister, Gina. The girls were the children of a doctor, who had left their mother and married their nanny. Their mother experienced significant depression, and due to this and their father's influence in the small community where they lived, he received full custody of the girls—Clare, Gina, and their middle sister, Jodi. Over time, I learned more about the situation that the girls had been living in with their father and stepmother. I was told that the stepmother was a practicing witch who abused the girls, withholding food and locking them in the bathroom. Clare was the strongest willed of the three sisters; at one point she was hospitalized, and the reports indicated bald spots where her hair had been pulled out. When Clare wouldn't submit to her parents, they focused the brunt of their abuse on the middle sister, Jodi. After her parents laced her food with pepper, Jodi asphyxiated, vomited, and choked to death. Not long after, Clare and Gina entered our home.

Clare quickly began having rages. When we were settling all of the children into their beds at night, she would ask for "fresh water." When Jim or I brought her a glass, she would throw it back at us, screaming that it wasn't "fresh enough." No responses would soothe her escalating rage. We visited a therapist and implemented suggestions that I now realize were more detrimental than helpful—for instance, we isolated her for a time in the lower level of the house. Knowing what we know now, I realize that the isolation likely only increased her cortisol levels, flooding her brain and making her even less coherent as her body's alarm bells amplified.

Ultimately, it was living in a calm, safe, structured environment that soothed Clare's raging amygdala and calmed her. Another factor was the court granting visitations with her mother. Initially, these visits reignited Clare's rages when her mother left again at their ends; her response was confusing at first, as there was no indication that her mother was part of the abuse she had experienced. Eventually, we determined that the trigger was the separation from her "safe" parent, and the trauma of that loss. Her mother began to stay with Clare until after she went to sleep, and the rages gradually subsided.

My time with Clare taught me about the huge impact of trauma, and about the need to keep trying different interventions until you find one that meets the needs of the child. Of course, all children, especially those who have experienced trauma, need a safe, calm, nurturing, structured environment. However, meeting the needs expressed through behavior, such as Clare's need for a gradual transition when her mother left, is critical to the healing process.

It is possible to make some informed guesses about the basic sources of trauma in a child's life. For example, a child who was removed from the home because his or her parents had a history of drug and alcohol abuse is likely to have a trauma history with substances. Environmental modifications, such as removing alcohol from the house, can go a long way toward making the environment feel safer to the child. However, to identify every distinct, individual source of trauma is an impossible task. Instead, what is essential is to be aware of the *presence* of trauma, and its connection to what we often think of as "bad" or unexplainable behaviors. The enduring task for a foster/adoptive parent or caregiver becomes to recognize the connection between certain behaviors and past trauma, rather than interpreting negative behaviors as intentionally hurtful or harmful.

*Attunement*

The detective work of understanding the sources of trauma can be facilitated through attunement, a concept taken from early attachment researchers such as John Bowlby. Daniel Hughes developed a psychotherapeutic treatment called Dyadic Developmental Psychotherapy in which he describes "inner subjectivity." By carefully attuning to the child's "subjective experiences" and responding with expressions, movement, gestures, and touch, Hughes is able to learn triggers, determine their sources, and help the child work through his or her response.

The roots of attunement and the reasons that it works are biological, and can predictably be found in the brain, in our mirror neurons. Imagine holding an infant in your arms. You scrutinize his tiny face. You widen your eyes, and he widens his eyes in return. You might stick out your tongue, and a newborn may mimic the gesture long before he has any ability to conceive of its meaning or significance. This is the work of mirror neurons in the brain, which help us to recognize and mimic the faces around us, to learn identification and empathy. There is evidence as well that mimicking or being "in-step" with others, practicing synchrony, helps to develop connection and empathy. Every culture in the world has its own dances, which serve to unite its people; the military still uses marching in-step and group exercises to build alliance and connect individuals (Szalavitz & Perry, 2010). Similarly, focused attention and synchrony build attachment between a caregiver and a child, encourage attachment, and help a caregiver to attune to the small reactions and behaviors in a child that indicate the presence of trauma.

In daily life, I think of the process of attunement as similar to tuning into a radio station, jiggling the knob until the station comes in. Essentially, by attuning to a child, you are closely observing, responding to emotions, connecting as completely as possible. I attune with my granddaughter by singing a song with her; I sing a line and then she repeats it; as I vary the songs, we must pay close attention to each other, becoming attuned through this kind of heightened connection.

Focused, face-to-face attention and responses are the foundation of attunement, which supports attachment and helps children to work through trauma as they feel the responsiveness of their parent or caregiver. If you are working hard to closely connect with a child, read his or her responses, and observe the ways that he interacts with the world, then the detective work of uncovering the sources and manifestations of trauma will begin to come naturally. When the child responds to a certain sound, smell, color, or tone and you are attuned to catch the response, you can continue to create a healing environment that grows more and more informed—and so more and more effective.

*Sensory Processing Disorder and Healing Trauma*

Over the last few years, it has become increasingly evident that many children who present with difficult behaviors are also struggling with sensory processing issues. I think it is important to include sensory issues in any discussion about recognizing behaviors as manifestations of trauma. Sensory Processing Disorder (SPD) is not new, but it has become increasingly recognized as a significant contributor to the many challenging behaviors of children "from hard places," as Dr. Karyn Purvis of Texas Christian University refers to them. An understanding of Sensory Processing Disorder can be another important tool in addressing the manifestations of trauma and helping children to heal.

We all learn through our senses; information comes into our brains through our eyes, ears, noses, mouths, and skin. Sensory processing is the way that we transform sensory information into messages we can act on, to give us a reliable picture of the world and our place within it. Right now, hopefully, your senses are working *together*. The majority of people are able to filter out unnecessary sounds and feelings; for instance, you filter out the feeling of your clothing, chair, and the floor beneath your feet. If a person occasionally loses focus because of an itchy shirt label, it may be due to a mild sensory issue. If, on the other hand, a person keeps sliding off the chair, looking toward sources of ambient noise, feeling like his shirt is painful, or seeing written words appear to pulse on paper, this may be Sensory Processing Disorder.

Sensory issues affect all kinds of people, from those with developmental delays, attention and learning problems, autism spectrum disorders, and other diagnoses to those *without any other issues*. SPD may affect a single sense, such as touch or sight, or it may be present in multiple senses. One child with SPD may over-respond to sensation; another child may under-respond and show little or no reaction to stimulation, extreme hot and cold, or even pain. In children whose sensory processing of messages from the muscles and joints is impaired, posture and motor skills can also be affected.

Indicators of Sensory Processing Disorder include out-of-proportion reactions to small touches, sounds, movements, tastes, or smells. A child may be bothered by clothing fabrics, or by tags or labels. He may be distressed by light or unexpected touches, dislike getting messy, or resist grooming. Often, a child with this disorder will be very sensitive to the volume or frequency of sounds. He may squint, blink, or rub his eyes frequently; he may be bothered by lights and patterns. He may have a high activity level, or be very sedentary; he may have an unusually high or low pain threshold.

The disorder can affect motor skills and body awareness, causing gross motor delays (walking, running, climbing stairs, catching a ball) or fine motor delays (using crayons, buttoning or snapping, beading, using scissors). A child with the disorder may have illegible handwriting, move awkwardly, or seem clumsy. He may have low or over-defined muscle tone. Similarly, oral motor and feeding problems can manifest, including oral hypersensitivity, frequent drooling or gagging, overly picky eating, and speech and language delays. In addition, these children often present with poor attention and focus, frequently "tuning out" or "acting up." They will often be uncomfortable or easily overstimulated in group settings. Many also struggle with self-confidence and independence.

Misdiagnosis is common with SPD, because the majority of health care professionals are not trained to recognize sensory issues. Effective treatment is available, but far too many children with sensory symptoms are misdiagnosed and not properly treated. Many children with behavioral problems are misdiagnosed with ADHD, or even Oppositional Defiant Disorder, when they are actually struggling with sensory integration issues. Most of these children are just as intelligent as their peers; many are intellectually gifted; their brains, however, are wired differently.

According to a groundbreaking new study from UC San Francisco, published in the online journal *NeuroImage: Clinical,* researchers have found quantifiable differences in brain structure, confirming a biological basis for the disorder that sets it apart from other neurodevelopmental disorders, such as ADHD and autism. Bunim (2013) writes that Mukherjee and Marco, the researchers behind the discoveries,

> "provide the first biological evidence that SPD is indeed a valid disorder, [demonstrating that] the abnormal microstructure of sensory white matter tracts shown by DTI (an advanced form of MRI called diffusion tensor imaging) in kids with Sensory Processing Disorder likely alters the timing of sensory transmission so that processing of sensory stimuli and integrating information across multiple senses becomes difficult or impossible."

The implication of these brain differences is that children with SPD need to be taught tools to help them process information. Once children with Sensory Processing Disorder have been accurately diagnosed, they benefit from a treatment program of occupational therapy with a sensory integration approach. In our detective work to find the root needs of our children in order to best help them to heal and become successful, I believe it is imperative that we consider the issue of sensory processing disorder as a causative factor in behavior challenges. The Sensory Processing Disorder Foundation states that Sensory Processing Disorder affects five to sixteen percent of children in the general population. Seeking services to appropriately evaluate our children is imperative in our process of providing them with what they need to begin to live their lives completely.

In our homes, working with a child with SPD begins by understanding his overreaction to sensory input, and understanding that his brain is wired in "fight or flight" mode the lion's share of the time. Let the child know that you understand that his issues are real, and that you are working on a concrete plan to help minimize his stress and sensory overload. We have talked at length in this chapter about the importance of identifying trauma triggers and recognizing behaviors as responses to triggers; for a child with sensory problems, it is even more critical to stay ahead of known triggers to minimize meltdowns. For a child with hypersensitivity to noise, try giving him a quiet place at home he can go to when he feels overwhelmed and needs a break. If your child has extreme sensitivity to certain types of clothing, purchase clothes that minimize this tactile overreaction. Many parents find weighted blankets, a "sensory diet," and activities such as swinging, rocking, and heavy lifting to be helpful. There are many resources that can help parents gain tools for working with a child with sensory integration issues. In particular, I have found Carol Kranowitz's (2005) *The Out-of-Sync Child: Recognizing and Coping with Sensory Processing Disorder* helpful. Recognizing, understanding, and staying ahead of your child's sensory issues by being prepared will go a long way toward minimizing distress and reducing outbursts and reactive behavior (Kranowitz, 2005).

*The Implications of Awareness*

At a training I was giving for parents recently, the children stayed with an intern in an adjoining room. A young boy crawled under a table and began to scream in the middle of the afternoon, seemingly without reason. The intern, standing above him, began to admonish him, but could not persuade him to stop. Leaving the training for a moment, I ducked under the table with him. I asked him if I could put my hand on him and when he replied affirmatively, I put my hand on his head. After rubbing his head for a few minutes, I asked him, "Can you stop screaming and just lay in here?"

The boy looked up at me and considered this. "Well, I'm cold," he said finally.

I took off my sweater and gave it to him. "If you feel like you have to scream again, can you just ask for Miss Nancy?" I asked him. Shortly afterward, he was out from under the table and playing with the group again.

This child's behavior, to a casual observer, was needlessly disruptive; it was "bad." However, when you look at this child through a trauma lens, his behavior was not a malicious attempt to wreak havoc on the intern and the other children, but rather a response to not feeling safe in a new environment. Working with populations who have experienced trauma, the beginning assumption should always be that behaviors have needs and traumas behind them. The shapes these behaviors take are varied and variable, but the existence of trauma is undeniable.

What does it mean, then, for caregivers to understand and respond to seemingly negative behaviors as the manifestations of early trauma, or to identify similar behaviors as sensory integration issues? For many foster/adoptive parents and caregivers, this knowledge can transform their experiences with children. Knowing that a child is exhibiting the effects of trauma, rather than acting with intentional antagonism, can change the caregiver's experience. More importantly, when a child's behaviors are met with understanding, protection, and nurture, the child can begin to heal in a real and enduring way. The implications of this healing may stretch across time, as well. Szalavitz and Perry (2010) write:

> Chronic, uncontrollable stress in early life can actually change gene expression, and these genes can be passed down from one generation to the next through alterations in parenting behavior. Being prepared for a stressful world increases aggression, while being prepared for a calmer world increases love. Again, this has huge implications... It is a mechanism by which the sins of the father can pass to the grandchildren and beyond. (p. 136)

So it follows that becoming aware and attuned to the sources of trauma does not only have an immediate effect for the child, but is also potentially brain-shaping and life-changing. A world in which the sources of trauma are recognized and addressed with intention and love will only continue to replicate itself across our lives and generations to follow.

# CHAPTER THREE

## LOUIS'S STORY: THE SIGNIFICANCE OF LOSS

My son, Louis, is now twenty-one years old, six feet tall, with dark hair and eyes and a shy smile. He is a student working toward a degree in health and athletic training, and last summer he married his high school sweetheart, a kind, animated blonde named Marie, at St. Patrick's Catholic Church.

What I know of Louis's life before he came into our family is like a series of blurry snapshots, vague memories of his youth that he has passed on to me. Born in Mexico, he lived there until he was seven or eight years old. He didn't live with his parents, but was passed from relative to relative. I picture his family as fairly well-to-do; Louis remembers a complex of homes, and an aunt he lived with more than any other relative. His young and still forming sense of self became intertwined with the way he was shuffled between relatives; he believed that he was being passed around because of his behavior, that he was an out of control child. He was sent to the United States to live with his uncle in Los Angeles, and then shortly sent on to South Bend, Indiana, to live with his mother and her abusive boyfriend. Eight year old Louis, a constant witness to terrifying violence, was at home during the fight that would change his life yet again; his mother slashed her boyfriend's throat, and Louis ran to a phone booth and dialed 911. He likely saved all three lives that day, but the result was his removal from the home and subsequent placement in foster care.

I begin this chapter by introducing my son Louis because in his story is a narrative of loss, of what was taken from him in each of his moves and how he came to heal. Pervasive and devastating loss is a significant issue in foster care and adoption. In fact, Fahlberg (1991) identifies the work of helping children to cope with traumatic losses and separations as one of the greatest challenges of the child welfare system. Every placement for a child, no matter how necessary or ultimately positive, is also a collection of losses, including the loss of his biological or former family, of friends, neighborhood, community, school, pets, familiar items, familiar places—the list goes on and on. Adoption for a foster child is the end of his hope of possible reunification with his biological parents, and a loss for the biological parents of the hope for their child ever returning home. Foster parents and families experience ongoing loss every time a child leaves the home. Often, foster parents don't recognize the impact of the accumulating losses on themselves, or on the other children in their home.

In this chapter, we will delve deeper into the scope of loss, and discuss ways to acknowledge and ameliorate some of the sorrow of traumatized children in order to ultimately help them to heal. Children experiences loss differently, but every child experiences loss. When I look at Louis, I see a young man who forged a life of love and connection out of the rubble of his losses, and I hope to offer some concrete strategies which can be used to support others to do the same.

*The Scope of Loss*

In the late nineteenth century, the United States was having growing pains. New York City was overcrowded; families lived in tenement houses in gruesome conditions, and thousands of abandoned, hungry children scrounged in the streets, often selling rags or matches, often erupting in violence, nearly always in poor health. At the same time, the West was beckoning—wide, unsettled land that was being painstakingly settled and worked as the railroads expanded westward. In this particular moment in time, Charles Loring Brace, a Methodist minister in New York City, proposed a unique solution—the neglected children, termed "street Arabs," would be put onto trains bound for the Midwest. Brace envisioned these children would be taken in and cared for by kind Christian families. The proposal was perhaps more practical than Brace's heartwarming projections suggest; while the children would presumably be cared for, they were simultaneously populating the wide and empty West, and providing an able workforce to develop the land ("The orphan trains," 1995).

Over 150,000 children were sent on trains bound for the Midwest between 1854 and 1929. They were "distributed" according to their usefulness; children were "put up" on stage and claimed; this is the origin of the phrase "put up for adoption." The oldest boys were chosen first, for their ability to work and to sleep in the barn; adolescent girls were chosen last because they were rumored to pose a threat to the woman of the house, and propriety required they be given rooms inside. Redheads and Catholics—the feared "others" at the time—similarly found themselves riding the trains farther and farther onward, passed up by families at each stop. The orphans were separated from siblings; they had no possessions or birth records. Appallingly, each train that left that East seemed to its passengers to be the only train; it wasn't until the 1960s and 1970s that the children who were "distributed" learned that they were part of a group that numbered into the hundreds of thousands (Kline, 2013).

The Charles Loring Brace project was the forerunner to the modern day foster care system, and the project's success remains ambiguous. While some children went on to experience lives of love and comfort, others endured abuse, or were treated simply as the help. However, the common thread between all of these children was the existence of significant loss. In the PBS documentary *The Orphan Trains*, a young girl writes from the comfort and luxury of her newly appointed home, "I would give a hundred worlds like this if I could see my mother" ("The orphan trains," 1995).

When I conduct trainings on adoption, I often begin by asking the question, "What is the first word that comes to mind when you think about adoption?" *Love*, people answer; they say *joy* and *blessings*. Instead, I tell them, "The first word I want you to think about is *loss*."

Loss is inherent in adoption and the adoption triad. Something negative has occurred for the child to be in the position of needing an adoptive family. The child has experienced the significant loss, even in infant adoption, of his or her birth family. With that comes loss of identity, loss of control, and loss of the extended biological family. For the biological family, adoption is the loss of their child, the dreams and hopes of their future with the child, and the childhood of their child. The adoptive parents are often building their family through adoption due to the loss of the dream of having biological children—the loss of having a child with their genetics, and the loss of the dreams they had for those children.

Louis's first foster parents went to our church and were friends of ours. Louis was a quiet young man, but his foster mother did a good job of facilitating his connection to his culture and his family, and for a while he had periodic phone calls with his mother and grandmother. When his mother was deported, the court terminated her parental rights, and Louis was moved to a pre-adoptive home. He lived in the pre-adoptive home for a school year, but the birth children and the foster mother in the home didn't like him. The foster father, on the other hand, did connect with Louis, but the division within the family was great, and eventually the family requested that Louis be moved.

In his second pre-adoptive home, Louis once again connected well to the foster dad, but it was while he was in this home that Louis learned that his mother had been killed. When I inquired about how Louis was doing, the response was "he's fine – he doesn't seem bothered by it." But Louis, a young man who internalized his feelings, acted out and got in trouble, and the family asked for him to be moved. As a result, Louis was sent to a residential program.

Tracing the skeleton path of Louis's placements, the losses add up quickly, hugely: the compounded losses of his mother, through separation, deportation, and finally death; the loss of his foster parents, particularly the losses of newly formed and potentially healing connections with the foster fathers in both homes; and the loss of his birth culture, his family culture, the cultures of his foster families, and each group of hard-won friends. From tenuous alliances to connections forged by blood and time, Louis was losing them all, over and over, carrying a burden of loss far too heavy for someone so young.

The program where Louis landed, after the death of his birth mother and his legal trouble, was on the residential campus where I was now overseeing the foster care program, so I would periodically see Louis. My children had remained connected to Louis, knowing him because his foster parents had been part of our church family. We had also been a respite home for him on several occasions. My children were actually the ones who came to me about Louis, saying, "Mom, you have to take him. He's a great kid, and you don't give up on kids." So we became the visiting family for Louis, and once he completed his time at the residential program he came into our home as a pre-adoptive placement.

## Louis's Story: The Significance of Loss

*Children in Placement*

An adoption specialist I know begins work with children in placement by saying, "Tell me about your losses." The behaviors displayed by a child in placement are created and provoked by the losses they have experienced—the birth family, schools, friends, pets, and on and on. They bring those losses into their subsequent homes.

To begin to address those losses, however, we must first define them and their effects. At the heart of all losses are disturbance, change, the disruption of connections, and the severing of ties that build emotional safety and stability. Consistency and security are keys to logical thinking and cause-and-effect connections. According to Fahlberg (1991), the impact of disturbance on a child is greatest between six months and four years, when children have learned to develop selective attachments, but have not yet learned that relationships can be maintained over distance or absence. When children are unable to attach to their caregivers in these early years, they develop the attachment issues we have talked about earlier in this book. Children may combat their fear that adults will leave them with clinginess and an arrested development, believing that if they show their age-appropriate skills, then their adults may abandon them to their own devices.

Alternately, children who have experienced the loss of their caregivers may begin to self-parent, withhold affection, and fail to attach. During the first three years of life in particular, children are susceptible to problems with their social development, and they often create magical scenarios—for instance, they may associate their bad behavior with the disappearance of a parent. These are crucial years for the development of a sense of right and wrong, and disruptions in these years may carry into adulthood (Fahlberg, 1991).

To talk about loss in the world of foster care and adoption is more often than not to talk about ambiguous loss, its many effects and manifestations. Ambiguous loss is as it sounds—loss that is indefinite and confusing, vague and hard to define. There are two main types of ambiguous loss. The first occurs when someone is psychologically present but physically missing. For example, if a child's parent is incarcerated, or he has been removed from his parent, that loss is one in which the parent is present in mind, but not in body. The second type, in contrast, occurs when someone is physically present but psychologically missing. For example, a child whose parent suffers from severe mental health or drug abuse issues may experience the emotional and psychological loss of a parent who still stands before him ("Understanding ambiguous loss," n.d.).

The greater the ambiguity of the loss, the more difficult it is to gain a sense of closure (Boss, 1999). In fact, there is rarely a clear "end date" for ambiguous losses. How long should a child mourn his or her birth family? What if a child never knew his birth family to lose them—what is appropriate then? When is the expiration date on wondering about a missing or drug-addicted parent? When should we "get over" things? The uncertain timeline of these traumatic ambiguous losses is even more profound because of the positive feelings associated with adoption. According to MN Adopt, a Human Services program of Minnesota, "a child may feel confusion or guilt over being asked to be happy that they were separated from their birth family. Extended family members and community may not recognize or understand that adoption is directly related to the loss of the original birth family" ("Understanding ambiguous loss," n.d.).

Ambiguous loss is often the most tangible in adolescence, when young adults are trying to establish their senses of identity. Ambiguous loss is marked by behaviors that intersect with attachment disorder and with PTSD—difficulty with transitions and decisions; an increasing inability to handle disappointment or smaller traumas; depression, anxiety, and guilt; and a myriad of other manifestations that resist an easy "fix."

When Louis came into our home, he was fifteen. He had experienced more loss and rejection than most people do in a lifetime. He had lost his country, his family, and his mother; he had been shuttled around in his birth family; he had been rejected by two pre-adoptive families. Although he had acted out some behaviorally, for the most part he internalized his anger. So, when he first came into our home he was a quiet, sullen young man who would, at times, have significant flare-ups. He resisted my attempts at nurturing him, countering them with strong internal walls. His resistance was often very hard for me because I wanted so much to help heal his hurt; when others saw him as moody and sullen, I saw him as incredibly hurting. And indeed, considering the path he had been down in such a short time in his life, it was easy to see that Louis was already haunted both by large concrete losses (homes, possessions) and by losses that were much more ambiguous but even more tremendous, the size of his mother and his country.

## *A Wider Lens: Loss in the Family*

Before we move on to discuss the ways that foster/adoptive parents can address loss in practice and work to help children to heal, I would like to take a moment to further acknowledge the depth and complexity of the other losses that hover over the adoptive triad.

### *The Biological Parents*

Loss is a significant issue for biological parents. The loss of a child to the system is often so devastating that the parent becomes nonfunctional, which can appear to the system as a lack of cooperation; in fact, many birth parents' coping skills are minimal, and the loss of their children becomes overwhelming.

In the last chapter, I talked about Clare and Gina, two sisters we fostered in the early 1990s, after the death of their middle sister. Following her divorce, Clare and Gina's birth mother went into a deep depression, which caused the court to grant the father full custody of their three daughters. After the death of the middle sister and the subsequent placement of Clare and Gina in our home, the mother had visits with her daughters in our home. I spoke in Chapter 2 about the rages Clare would have, and how we eventually realized they coincided with her mother leaving. To address the trauma, the mother would stay in our home while her daughter fell asleep—sometimes a vigil of hours. During this time, I would sit and speak with the mother. She was struggling with the loss of her daughter, her feelings of having failed to protect her child, and her guilt for her absence and for not knowing that the abuse was occurring. In addition, she was living through the loss of her two remaining daughters to foster care and potentially to one of the sets of grandparents, who were all embroiled in a custody battle. I witnessed the incredible sadness she was experiencing through the months the girls lived with us, as well as her incredible ability to support her girls and eventually achieve her goal of having them come and live with her.

The tremendous loss that birth parents experience when their children are removed from their home is often met with a primal response: fight, flight, or freeze. Some parents respond by becoming very angry toward the foster parent, the case manager, and the child welfare system. Others freeze and seem to have no ability to do what is being asked of them by the court. Others just give up and flee, running from the situation through lack of compliance and lack of involvement with their child. But the system – judges, case managers, foster parents, and so on--don't see this as a loss response; they view it as noncompliance. That negative view of the birth parent leads to criticism and a dismissal of the birth parents' emotions. When birth parents' emotions and experiences are validated, many are able to become cooperative with the process of their children returning home and more accepting of the services provided to them to assist the process.

*The Foster Family*

In twenty-three years, Jim and I had one weekend when we didn't have a foster child with us at home. Children came in and out of our home and our lives. It was easy to dismiss the impact on Jim and me and the core family (our biological children and those we had adopted), because we weren't the ones leaving or being shuttled elsewhere. I still remember, however, my youngest biological son turning to me once and asking when he would have to go; the impact of loss had fueled his certainty that one day it would be his turn to leave.

Foster parents and families experience ongoing loss every time a child leaves the home. Many, times foster parents don't recognize the impact of this. It is critical to address these losses and utilize coping skills to manage the losses not only for the foster parents, but for the entire foster family. This generally involves intentionally discussing feelings with the children in the family and finding safe people for the foster parents to talk to. When a child leaves there is the sense of loss, but also, depending on the child, sometimes a sense of relief and peace back in the home. These feelings also need to be processed because often the other children (and the parents) may feel a sense of relief when a child leaves, while at the same time feeling guilty for having these feelings. Many of the strategies for addressing loss in the foster family are similar to those we will talk about in the next section, as we begin to consider how to help children heal from both ambiguous and concrete losses.

*Overcoming Loss: Strategies and Interventions*

Children cannot handle separations and losses without supportive help. Grief is the process of overcoming loss, and children cannot grieve until their losses have first been affirmed. It is important that children receive reassurance from adults that it is possible and natural to feel strong and often contradictory emotions about people they don't often see (Fahlberg, 1991).

One of the most basic strategies for helping children to overcome loss, particularly ambiguous loss, is to give voice to it. We live in a culture that often encourages us to "keep a stiff upper lip" and manage our sorrows alone, but for traumatized children, this strategy will only arrest the healing process. Adopted children need permission to feel contradictory things—sorrow at the loss of their birth family, relief, joy, anger, and so on. They need the freedom to feel these things and to speak about them without guilt or the sense that sorrow for their losses at all detracts from the love of their new family. They need to be able to talk about their grief, and to have their feelings heard and validated.

Similarly, incorporating losses into rituals, and acknowledging the pieces of a child's life that have come before—rather than pretending that prior life and those losses didn't exist—can be a powerful tool to help a child heal. For example, creating a memory box, or helping the child to perform a certain ritual of remembrance, or doing things as simple as mentioning the child's birth family on important days such as holidays and birthdays, all go a long way toward combating the invisibility and lack of acknowledgement that feed ambiguous losses.

When possible, another significant element in addressing loss is acknowledging the importance of the biological family. The connection that exists in bio-families is powerful, and if we deny that loss, or erase that relationship in situations where it is safe and possible to maintain, then we are not understanding the needs of the child.

I remember clearly my son Eric's struggle with the losses he suffered. We spoke of Eric in the first chapter of this book. He had an ongoing relationship with his grandparents, and sometimes went on visits with his father. Still, he had a hard time managing two families; it was clear that he felt conflicted over contradictory emotions and what he perceived as clashing loyalties. When he was twelve, Eric fell ill, and I took some time off of work to have the opportunity to care for him. I took him to a physician and while he was lying on the exam table he sighed dramatically, "When I die, give everything to my real family!"

I replied, "Eric, what about your grandmother?"

"She's my real family," he said.

"Eric," I told him, "first of all, she is your step-grandmother, so she is as blood-related to you as I am. Real is the person who cares for you—so we are both your real family."

He shrugged and said, "Okay—you can each have half." Although his response was his usual, unintentionally flip style, I think the conversation made an impact on him, and he began to understand that "real" is about who cares for you. When working with children who have experienced these kinds of losses, it is essential for them to be allowed the freedom to let their losses and loves coexist—to know that continuing to love the parents they have been taken from, or to long for people they no longer see, is not at odds with the new future they are creating.

Above all else, it is essential that children not be made to feel that there is any certain timeline on their losses. There is no clear cure or certain timeline, and the losses never entirely disappear. None of these strategies is a clear poultice to apply to loss—none of them ensures a certain result. But by acknowledging the child's losses and allowing them to coexist in the child's life with his or her new joys, a space is made for grief and for healing.

I don't believe Louis talked much about his losses with his therapist, although his therapist didn't include me much as a foster parent. Over time, Louis began to open up and share with me more and more. Often, these conversations took place late at night, when he was having difficulty sleeping. I believe that I can count two times when I had to correct Louis's behavior; I tried very hard to not internalize his moodiness and love him unconditionally with very minimal correction or negative statements. The time in our lives that brought Louis and me closer was when we established his citizenship. When we adopted Louis, we were told that once he was the legal child of a United States citizen, he would automatically be granted citizenship. But this was not the case. We spent long days en route to Indianapolis to visit an immigration attorney, and shared many negative experiences. The final outcome, however, was positive—his citizenship—and the challenges we went through together ultimately built our relationship and made it much stronger.

Louis did respond better to Jim, who engaged him in activities; Louis is a person who likes working with his hands and keeping busy. I mentioned previously that the work projects Louis and Jim did together had a future payoff, too, in that Louis now gets lots of odd jobs, like painting, laying floors, and dry walling. I believe time, unconditional love, and acceptance have helped in Louis's process of healing, which is ongoing. His greatest source of healing has been through Marie, his wife. She has given Louis unconditional love, and because of that he has been able to share his thoughts, feelings, and experiences with her.

Louis still struggles with the trauma of his past. He still struggles with sleeping and bouts of discouragement. He does not want to reconnect with his biological family, although we have offered to go with him. His fear of losing Marie causes him to smother her, at times. At the same time, he brings great strengths to his relationships—unconditional acceptance, care for his family, and an intuitive understanding of the needs of others.

I relate these ups and downs with Louis to demonstrate how circuitous the path out of loss can be. There is no magic spell, no miracle cure. And yet, over time, and with continued intention, healing does begin to take place.

*Final Thoughts*

In *Macbeth,* Shakespeare writes, "Give sorrow words; the grief that does not speak knits up the overwrought heart and bids it break."

This is the biggest command of loss—to let it speak, to acknowledge it and not try to dismiss it. To dismiss loss is to dismiss the child's lived experiences, and the fact that those experiences have made him the person that he is today. And over time, with that acknowledgment, healing will occur.

Perhaps the turning point for some of Louis's healing from so much loss was when we bought him a puppy. He had just started dating Marie, and her dog had puppies. He asked if we could adopt one. I wasn't excited about another puppy, but I agreed. My heart overflowed with joy as I watched Louis love and nurture the puppy. I will always remember a fall afternoon when I was raking leaves in the yard, and I watched Louis take off his sweatshirt and wrap it around his puppy as she slept nearby. I knew then, watching how Louis was able to give so much love to his puppy, that my son was healing.

# CHAPTER FOUR

## THE RELATIONSHIP OR THE BATTLE? BUILDING ATTACHMENT THROUGH INTENTION AND UNCONDITIONAL LOVE

Allen came into our home on borrowed time. His sister, who was living in the foster home of a good friend of mine, asked me and his caseworker to give him "one more chance" before he was sent to

Boy's School. Allen entered our home the summer before his 8th grade year in high school, wearing sagging pants and a sour disposition. I agreed to take him.

Allen's story is one of great intention. He came into our home very angry, and we encouraged him to start fresh, to be whoever he wanted to be. I remember him in those early days, when he decided, in our community where no one knew him, that he wanted a "preppy" look; we shopped and bought a new "preppy" wardrobe. Allen agreed to abide by my one rule about his wardrobe—that he had to have and wear a belt.

Allen was a quiet, reticent young man. It was difficult at times for me because he did not seem to receive my love well. I knew he needed to attach, but he was characteristic of many teens; he was developmentally pulling away, just as I was trying to build attachment. He was a young man who avoided physical touch. Often I would sit next to him in church so that we were touching arm to arm, in order to have some contact with him.

Allen's room was across the hall from Eric's room, which would prove to be a blessing; the boys were in the same grade, and Eric became a strong role model for Allen. Allen was also able to rise to the challenge of having academically gifted brothers in the house, and was able to gradually do well in school. His anger would still erupt at times. He frequently bullied one of our younger sons, and he had little tolerance for younger children in general; I would sometimes have to stop the van until he would stop picking on the younger children. Once, when Jim was driving, the bullying became so insufferable that I left the van with Allen and we walked. As we walked, I tried to process with him about how what he was doing was hurting others, and to help him understand the need for everyone to feel safe in our family. Once he had calmed down, Jim picked us up and we went home. I knew that yelling at Allen or returning his level of anger was not going to model for him what I wanted. He responded well to talking and being allowed the normalcy of teenage activities.

Football and weightlifting became Allen's sources of joy. I learned the game of football because I wanted to know what I was watching when I would sit with Allen and watch games on television. More importantly, when I went to his games, I wanted to understand the game enough to talk with him about it. Football gave him an outlet for his anger and the discipline he needed for success. By his junior year, he was becoming an increasingly responsible young man. We asked the judge if he could get a driver's license, and this request was granted. Allen was working, and we helped him buy a car. His car was very important to him, and he knew he had to maintain his job, behavior, and grades to keep it.

When Allen was a senior, his caseworker came to our home. I had asked her to visit Allen in our home; he was very embarrassed to have a caseworker visit him at school. School visits were her normal practice, but Allen didn't like looking different or fielding questions from his peers after she left. The caseworker, a stoic brunette, sat on our couch, between Allen and me. "So, what do you do to discipline Allen?" she asked.

"I talk to him," I answered.

"Surely you have to do more than that," she said.

"Allen is a very responsible, responsive young man, and he responds to us discussing things that I have concerns about," I replied.

She turned to Allen, raising her eyebrows. "Is that correct?"

"Yeah," Allen said, shrugging.

The caseworker looked like she didn't believe either of us, but most children and young adults, given a consistent atmosphere of calm, trust, and respect, will respond to discussing issues. A good conversation is conducive to responsiveness in a way that lecturing and plaintive cries of *Why?* are not constructive, and may in fact be detrimental and relationship-damaging.

I still think of those early days, when Allen was putting on his new collared shirts, trying on his new self, in many ways. Five years later, Allen was the football team captain, and I was a very proud mom, walking on the field with him on Senior Night. His football coach told me that night that he had never seen a young man change as much in four years as he had seen Allen change, and complimented me for that. There were so many factors in Allen's transformation: our family's influence and the unconditional love I tried hard to give him; football; the mentoring that our son Eric, who was in the same grade, provided; and Allen's fierce desire to be successful. However, all of those influences were driven by intention, by careful choices to prioritize our relationship.

Creating this kind of atmosphere, and being intentional in the string of ongoing moments that make up months and years of life with traumatized children requires great intention; however, I realize that it is not as simple as saying, "do it." The daily experience of working with traumatized children is full of moments of high emotion. In this chapter, we'll talk in depth about how to leverage these difficult moments into opportunities for leading with love and creating an environment of safety and connection.

*Relationships in Practice*

In the winter of 2008, we took a family trip to Gulf Shores, Alabama, for Christmas. Boats strung with lights bobbed in the harbor. The beach was a long and serpentine, bone-colored, dotted with clumps of tousled grass. We spent a lot of time together as a family that Christmas, playing board games in the main room of the rental condo, cooking in the sparse kitchen. There was a lot of laughter—and eventually, a lot of cabin fever.

One of the cardinal rules for foster parents is that foster youth are to be supervised at all times, but as sophomores in high school, our boys Jay and Louis sought to have normal teenage experiences. One afternoon, they asked to go down the street to purchase shirts at a souvenir shop—one of the many storefronts offering a jumble of seashell art, screenprinted t-shirts, and beachscape postcards. I gave them an hour to go and return.

It was three hours and many unreturned texts and calls later when Jay and Louis returned to the rental condo. My fear was compounded by something that had happened the summer before, when Jim was home with the kids. He had run to the hardware store, and during the thirty minutes that he was away, Louis's probation officer came by the house, finding him "unsupervised." Our 18-year-old son, Alex, was home, but the probation officer didn't consider this to be acceptable. She threatened to move Louis if we didn't supervise him properly. As I called Louis's phone and the voicemail picked up yet again, my heart was pounding both from the fear of what might have happened that day, but also because of an even darker fear—the idea that I could lose Louis, that such a small moment could come to define all of our lives.

I dialed both Louis's and Jay's cell phones over and over. When they returned, looking sheepish, it was two hours later than they were supposed to be home. I was upset; I was worried; I was angry. As foster parents and caregivers, we are often faced with moments like these, when we need to choose: the relationship, or the battle?

The most recent research on happiness points to the source of our greatest joy being relationships, and the only way to assure happiness is through relational behavior. Our relationships are what heal us, and what sustain us (Szalavitz & Perry, 2010). Even in anger and fear, it is essential that our focus be on relationships, on building them through intentional, loving relational behavior. But how do you do this in practice? How do you do this when your two teen boys show up, two hours late, and your heart is in your throat? How do you do this when you want—need—them to understand that the behavior is not okay?

When Jay and Louis walked in, I was crying. My emotions were overwhelming: I was experiencing breathless relief, happiness, frustration. "If I don't know where you are," I kept saying, "I can't keep you safe. I love you so much, and I couldn't bear to lose you. I need to know where you are. I get so scared, because I love you so much." If they were just anyone, I told them, I wouldn't care where they were, or why they didn't come back on time—but they were my sons, and my first job was to keep them safe. I was crying, holding them to me. I held them for both the boys and myself—for the ocean of relief that was crashing over me, and because attachment is built in times of high emotion. Anger and accusations would have damaged our relationship, but my response and my words of affirmation, even at that level of emotion—perhaps because of the level of emotion—were instead evidence of my care and concern. I could have lit into them for what they had done. In that moment, I had an opportunity to act with intentionality, to use the experience to further our relationships, rather than to harm them.

In these situations, our impulse is often to demand, "Why?": *Why won't you listen to me? Why did you skip class? Why were you smoking?* As counterintuitive as it *feels*, I think that we can remove the word "Why" from our vocabulary when we are communicating with teenagers. "Why" solicits the response "I don't know," or a fabricated story—what they think you want to hear, what they think it will take to remove the pressure. When I'm working with foster parents or caregivers, I often ask them if they know that fast food French fries are bad for them. Invariably, they answer that they do. "And do you still—once in a while—still eat them?" I ask. Most of them admit that they do. "Why?" I ask them. "*Why* do you do that?" They shrug sheepishly. We can't always explain why we do things, and teens have decidedly less impulse control or ability to name and describe their emotions; "Why?" is only a question that leads to frustration and works against the relationship.

While we can't always control the why of our children's behavior, we can be intentional in specific and practical ways, to ensure that even in anger, we don't damage carefully forged relationships. Attachment and intention are inextricably linked.

A major way to always keep the relationship in focus, even during the worst battles, is to couch everything in safety. As a parent or caregiver, many of the big battles are actually about safety. We want to know where our children are, not to ruin their fun, but to make sure that we can keep them safe. If a teen breaks curfew and the caregiver is upset because the child "didn't listen," and "was out getting into trouble when you should have been home," that is a response that undermines attachment. However, if the caregiver is upset because he or she "was worried about what might have happened, and how I couldn't keep you safe," that is a response that comes from love and shows the child how much he or she means to the caregiver. With practice, we can easily shift our tendency to angrily ask "Why?," to instead say, "I love you so much, and so it upsets me when I think you may not be safe."

Using a "Time In," rather than a "Time Out," is another important practice. Keeping a child with you after he or she misbehaves sends a clear message that your relationship is not being compromised by the child's behavior. In our house, we had a sturdy chair with arms; children could scrape or wiggle; "Time In" was about getting oneself back under control, as opposed to enduring a certain amount of punishment or time. I didn't want kids to be isolated in their bedrooms during times of high emotion; instead, during a meltdown they would know that I was with them, helping them.

I also found that there were battles I chose not to engage in at all. For example, I see many foster/adoptive parents fall apart over issues with food. Food is a way for children to exercise control over their days, and it is also a challenge that presents itself as many as three or four times a day. This is a battle I chose not to fight—a battle I didn't want to have. My son Dimitri went to Ecuador in college, and we joked that it was the first time that he ate anything green. There may have been truth in that; food wasn't something I was willing to make an issue. School, similarly, is often a point of contention between foster parents or caregivers and children. There is a focus these days on involving parents in education. Often, schools ask or expect parents to intervene when it comes to problems that have occurred during the school day, or to enforce accountability with homework. However, my perspective has always been that if the problem is at school, the school needs to handle it, to be the enforcer. I can give a child time to do his or her homework, but I am not going to fight battles over school at home. I think this is a task for every parent or caregiver: Part of your job is to determine what your big battles are, and to ask yourself if those are safety issues and if they are worth risking your relationship with the child. If they are worth intervention—worth the fight, in other words—then the task becomes how to handle the issue while keeping the relationship at the forefront.

*Emotional Regulation & the Value of Reparation*

Letting go of the things that aren't important may be easy when it comes to battling over broccoli or a messy room. However, in times of high emotion, when we as caregivers feel out of control, it can be easy to fly off the handle. How many of us have heard another parent in the moment of explosion, when a calm, measured voice gives way to "How many times have I told you not to do that?"

Everyday stresses can be challenging for parents, but as caregivers working with traumatized children, the behavioral manifestations of trauma that we discussed in Chapter 3 may be especially difficult to manage. We spoke about Eric in Chapter 2, and about our long work on attachment. Eric's older brother, Alex, was exceptionally challenging for me. He was cruel to animals, inappropriately touched children, and would complete chores in a way that made things look remarkably worse. His disrespect for me, coupled with his positive warmth toward Jim, made me—and others—question my sanity. I would find myself wanting to scream.

Children exposed to trauma have a difficult time regulating their emotions; their moods are variable. They have difficulty knowing and describing their emotions and internal states. Adult emotional regulation becomes even more important; it is much easier for a child to feel safe and to attach to an adult who provides consistent and steady love and protection. When I would disregulate, I was coming apart for the whole family, losing hard-won ground in my attachment with these children. At that time, in 1992, we had two girls staying with us. Lynn and Rachelle were eleven and seventeen, and in their fifth placement. Lynn, who was very close to me, said, "Mom, you never yelled until Alex and Eric moved in." Together, she and I decided that she would cue me with the word "chill" when she saw me becoming disregulated. This allowed me to remember that my job was to stay on an emotional even keel, to practice emotional regulation so that the children could feel safe.

Emotional regulation kept me consistent, enabling me to be able to step back and look at a child's behavior as a manifestation of experience, rather than purposeful antagonism. I worked with a child who had been horribly abused in a satanic ritual. When he was eleven, he started a house fire and was subsequently hospitalized. He was quiet, nearly silent; the only time he expressed emotion was on paper, when his social worker asked him to write down an emotion, and later two emotions, in a day, in exchange for a snack reward. His foster parents took him home after his time in the hospital, and one day the foster mother called to say, "Michael yelled at me! I'm so excited!" That progress—from the child's silence to the mother's excitement—is a direct and therapeutic result of a child trusting enough to share his emotions with an adult who is emotionally regulated enough to manage that sharing. Michael's foster mom saw that his ability to finally express emotion was far more significant than issues of perceived disrespect.

Of course, not every conflict can be easily navigated and managed with emotional regulation, and sometimes, regardless of our intention, we find ourselves in conflict. The greatest conflict I had was with my son Eric, during his senior year in high school. He was dating a girl who was very possessive of him. The relationship seemed one-sided; she never came to our house or participated in any of our family activities. She would only go on dates with Eric in my car, not wanting to be seen in our ten-passenger van. Eric was still doing well in school, sports, and active in church youth group, but I still felt that he wasn't being treated well.

We held Eric's open house on the day of his high school graduation, so that his biological family from out-of-town could attend both events. After the graduation, everyone gathered at our house to celebrate: Eric, his girlfriend, his biological family and our family, and other friends and guests. After about an hour, Eric announced that he had to leave. When I asked him why, he said he had to attend his girlfriend's grandmother's birthday party.

When Eric returned later that evening, around 11 p.m., I was upset with him; I was hurt and angry that he had chosen to attend the birthday party rather than to spend time with his guests and relatives.

It was one of two times I remember getting very upset with Eric, and he left the house and didn't return until 2:00 a.m. By that point, I was frantic that he was safe, and I resolved that I was going to approach the situation and his relationship with his girlfriend differently. When he came home I apologized for being so emotional, and I told him that I loved him, no matter what.

Eric's relationship with his girlfriend lasted into his sophomore year of college, and it caused distance between us off and on, particularly after our family moved east and he continued to return to our old home town on weekends to see his girlfriend, rather than visiting the new house. But relationships are long games, and what mattered most was that I continued to let him know that I loved him and was concerned for him. I wanted him to understand that my love for him did not diminish, regardless of conflict or circumstances.

Eric and I refer today to the evening of the open house as "our fight." Despite being upset with him earlier on, I was able to reframe my reactions, to emotionally regulate, and to show him that my love was unconditional, that night and over time. While in an ideal world, conversation will eliminate conflict, these emotional moments can still be an opportunity to demonstrate that conflict is not equal to the end of a relationship, and that conflict does not negate love. Even though we don't always handle situations as we'd like to, and we can't always emotionally regulate with the kind of ease we aim for, the most powerful impact we can have on someone is to love them unconditionally, and to remind them of that through our words and actions.

*Loving Unconditionally*

The conflict that Eric and I experienced is one that strengthened our relationship in the long-term, and since his relationship with his then-girlfriend ended, we no longer experience contention over it. However, loving unconditionally is not a conditional practice. One of the most important experiences I have had with loving unconditionally has been with my son DeShawn.

DeShawn came into our home at the age of sixteen. He had been placed in foster care when he was thirteen, due to his home situation. He and his older brother had originally been placed together, but they were separated after getting into some trouble; DeShawn was sent to a residential program, and his brother, an excellent basketball player, was placed in a different foster home, so he could continue to play for his high school. DeShawn did well at his residential program, and they were looking for an African American foster home for him; however, the "delinquent" label he carried proved a stumbling block for placement. I asked if I could meet him, and immediately saw his kind heart and need for a good home environment.

DeShawn was the same age as Eric and Allen, but a year behind them in school; with an IQ of 69, he was enrolled in special education. He struggled some in school and in his behavior choices. It seemed that so many of his choices were due not so much to his IQ, but poor cause-and-effect thinking and boundaries. His lack of boundaries often extended to stealing, or, more aptly, taking things from the family which weren't his; if he needed something, he would take it. There was no use in asking DeShawn if he took something – he would just say "no," despite evidence to the contrary. Now, years later, I think he feels safe enough to say that he did take something, but rather than asking, as a family we all learned to use environmental modification—we don't leave things where they might become a temptation. I remember one Christmas, during his freshman year in college, I gave my oldest son gift cards for Christmas. When they disappeared, instead of confronting DeShawn about stealing, he said "I should have known better than to leave them out where he could be tempted to take them." By removing the temptations, we all worked to help DeShawn be successful. The emphasis in our family became on supporting each other's successes.

During the time he lived with us, DeShawn stayed on track; when we moved, he was starting his senior year in high school, and he was able to enroll in the high school connected to his previous residential program. With individualized support, he was able to earn a high school diploma. DeShawn's transition into adulthood has not made him any less of a part of our family, and the challenges have also continued. DeShawn has been off-and-on involved with drugs and alcohol, and the subcultures that surround those substances. He has been in jail twice and lost his driver's license for six years due to two DUI's. He continues to take things from us without asking. He has two children by women who were both one night sexual experiences.

Sometimes, I think it is confusing to people as I describe my family. I have a doctor son, a son who is a health and safety manager, a Green Beret son, a computer whiz son, an engineer son, and a son in college, and then I have a son who inconsistently works, doesn't pay child support for his daughter, and has two children outside of marriage (or even a relationship). I have been asked by people why I keep involved in DeShawn's life. I am somewhat offended by that question. He is my son. I don't approve of his behavior, but I love and accept him because of our relationship. When he is making good choices, he is a kind and giving person, a good dad, and a good son. I know that about him and reinforce that to him. When he is not making good choices, I try to keep connected to him and love him through those periods. All the boys are able to love and accept DeShawn, no matter what. Eric has struggled some with DeShawn's choices, however, as he recognizes that DeShawn's children are our grandchildren and his son's cousins, he is beginning to soften up, to extend the bounds of his own love and acceptance. What I do know is that DeShawn needs a mom, a dad, and a family, which he now has; of all of my children, DeShawn has taught me that my relationship to him is more important than anything I own. His children are the delights of my life.

My newest opportunity for loving is DeShawn's fiancé. She has been to our house a few times but is very quiet, and has three cute kids. She seems hesitant to connect, so it appears that I have my work cut out to convince her that I care for her and accept her unconditionally. I have never seen DeShawn this in love and committed to a girl before, so I am up to the challenge; building relationships and attachment is a never ending job!

*Toward a Relational Future*

Cedar Lake is a small, scenic town in northwestern Indiana, established by pioneers in the mid-19th century. The lake itself is the largest natural lake in the area, and it is surrounded by hills and clusters of houses jockeying for lake access. Like many smaller communities, there is a large disparity between high and low incomes, between the tony upper-class homes and the dilapidated housing caused by people turning century-old lake cottages into living spaces.

My sister is the director of the Cedar Lake Library, where she runs a very successful teen group. Youth gather to play games and socialize during latchkey hours, when teens tend to be susceptible to risky behavior out of boredom and a lack of supervision. One of the teen boys in the group painted a bright, slashing graffito on the library's stone and brick exterior. My sister was instructed to call the police and report the vandalism, and also to suspend him from the library for a month. My sister agreed that there needed to be a consequence, but she also wanted to have him paint—artistically— the teen room when he returned. She thought that if he could use his talent in a positive way, he would receive a lot of praise and reinforcement. Unfortunately, the answer was a resounding no.

Our society has come to view tough love as a solution. A bully "needs a taste of his own medicine," or we should show no lenience for bad behavior. While consequences are vital part of raising a child, the tough love ideology has "failed to recognize our fundamental need for connection" (Szalavitz & Perry, 2010, p. 304). By shutting down my sister's plan for the teen room mural, the library was choosing the battle over the relationship, instituting a relationship-ending consequence instead of taking advantage of a relationship-building opportunity.

However, the young man continues to come to the library. He comes to visit my sister, standing at the reference desk to speak to her. I spoke with her about her fear that even with her support, he would begin using drugs or be incarcerated, like the other members of his family. I understand that fear, the sense of hopelessness in the face of what seems like a losing battle against the specters of trauma.

However, resiliency studies continuously show that what makes a difference is one person in a child's life who has unconditional, positive regard for the child over a long period of time. In other words, my sister's presence in this young man's life, the consistent and positive nature of that relationship, is not insignificant; in fact that relationship might make all the difference. With her, he has a good, safe place to come, and a consistently positive person to greet and support him.

    As caregivers, we have opportunities every day to choose to be those consistently positive people. We can choose to value relationships over battles, to provide a safe environment through our emotional regulation, and to "discipline by reasoning, perspective taking, consistency of appropriate consequence, and above all, love" (Szalavitz & Perry, 2010, p. 313). By doing this, we show our children that our love is unconditional and unwavering, and we allow them the safety to begin to love us in return.

# CHAPTER FIVE

## INTERDEPENDENT LIVING

On my desk is a family photograph, taken two years ago. There are sixteen of us in the photograph, comprising two haphazard rows. The youngest are drawn into the laps of other family members. Each family, I know, has its own unique composition, and ours is no different: there is Allen on the outside, because he is generally the least connected. Alex and Dimitri are toward the middle, although Eric is still the spark of the group. Louis ducks down, because he has never been comfortable having his picture taken. Jim doesn't push toward the middle, but I can see how happy he is to be part of the melee. I'm generally in the middle, where I can be surrounded by so many people that I love—and also hide my stomach. Ivan is, as always attempting to do "bunny ears"—even at the age of 26.

This photograph, like any photograph of our family, is striking for many reasons. The diversity of ages, sizes, and races, for one—and beyond that, the diversity of personalities and histories that may be less obvious to someone who isn't familiar. Each photograph that is taken of our family is a visual testament to one of our most important characteristics—that our family is not static, but continues to grow, even as we have stopped bringing in new foster children. I see our family like a celestial body that pulls others into its orbit through the force of interconnectivity. There are DeShawn's children, from two different mothers; Louis's wife holds one of them while I hold the other. Now, in 2014, Jim and I have no children who are still our legal dependents at home, but the fact that they have launched into new lives, relationships, cities, and schools does not mean that they have left us. Our family continues to grow in unexpected ways, and we sustain and support each other. This photograph is a visual manifestation of my family's dance of connection, and the fallacy of independence as the indicator of success.

In this chapter, we will discuss how our biology drives our need for connectivity, and the challenges that the foster care system faces in supporting children, particularly older youth who are grappling with the transition to adulthood. We'll also continue to consider how we can put this knowledge into practice, and move toward a stronger system and future for our families.

*The Biology of Connection*

Throughout this book, we have demonstrated how humans are social creatures—how we thrive from touch, from connection, from attention. Our social connections begin in utero, and continue to branch and build as our caregivers look into our just-open eyes, mirroring our emotions, exercising and shaping our stress responses, providing us with language and its meaning. There is evidence that our ability to share childcare—to raise our children in empathic systems and to care for children who are not biologically our own—has propelled the human species forward. Our altruism and our interconnectivity have ensured our survival and created our capacity for happiness (Perry & Szalavitz, 2010).

Additionally, the quality and number of our relationships directly correlates with our resilience. In their book *Born for Love*, Perry and Szalavitz (2010) devote an entire chapter to Iceland, which measures among the highest birth rates, lowest rates of infant mortality, and highest measurements of happiness of all nations in the world. Interestingly, Iceland also has a high divorce rate, but the effects of these separations and losses on children are nearly negligible. This is because the tiny island nation is comprised of close networks of family and friends. In a community of intense interdependence and interconnectivity, individual separations do not have the same damaging effect that they do in a country like the United States, where the isolated nuclear family is the norm (Perry & Szalavity, 2010).

The extolling of independence—the idea that we should be able to cope on our own, all by ourselves, is a uniquely modern and even a uniquely American idea. This model gained even more ground in the 80s and 90s, replacing the intergenerational, "it takes a village" family model. The model states that we should not seek solace in our relationships or our communities; rather, we should have everything we need within ourselves. The model insists that success is about not being dependent, not asking for help; when you can meet all your needs without reliance, then you have arrived.

The idea that independence equals success means that we are measuring ourselves against our ability to provide and thrive alone, and to maintain complete autonomy in our relationships. We are telling ourselves and our children that when we ask for help, when we look to each other for kindness, when we share each other's happiness and sorrow, we are failing. We are born needing each other to learn to cope with stress, but in this model of independence, we are telling ourselves and our children that to be successful is to work against their very biology. The fallacy of independence is harming precisely the people it promises to help.

*A Faulty System*

Lynn was eleven years old when she moved in with our family. She was a headstrong blonde, smart and brassy, loving and needy. I've spoken of her earlier in this book; she was the child who built her attachment with me by crawling into my lap as I fed my youngest son, and later she helped me to practice intention and emotional regulation, giving me cues when my own reactions to other children became motivated by frustration and a feeling of helplessness. In the 1990s, there was a lot of systemic reluctance around moving to the permanency plan of adoption, and so we were never able to adopt her, but she and I were nonetheless exceptionally close.

Lynn turned seventeen in the summer before her senior year in high school, a balmy Indiana summer that went on and on. She fell in love that summer, with an older man who was deeply involved in using and trafficking substances. By early fall, she had been arrested. I requested that she receive some services to help her to get back on track, but instead of mandating outpatient services and returning her to our home, the judge sent her to a residential program. She promptly ran away; the judge decided then to send her home, to a father who had been convicted of selling her older sisters to truck drivers on the Indiana toll road. He spent only one and a half years in jail. In the five and a half years that Lynn lived with our family, she visited her parents only once. As per the judge's mandate, Lynn returned home. She ran away shortly after, became homeless, and has never obtained her high school diploma or her GED.

Lynn's story has a happy ending; she eventually became a wonderful mother, and she has a committed relationship with the father of her children. I'm proud of the life she has chosen to lead. At the same time, Lynn's story is a reflection of the struggles of the child welfare system.

Lynn's story is one of the failure of the system, rather than her own failure. To place a seventeen-year old back in the home of convicted child molester while saying, from the bench, "She is old enough to take care of herself," is an example of a child welfare system that is not about success but about reducing numbers. Lynn was done a tremendous disservice by the same systems that were theoretically designed to serve her. I am confident that if she had received more appropriate and comprehensive services, she would have completed high school and not had the struggles that she had in her early adulthood—not have had to fight her way forward against quite so much resistance.

Lynn's story is all too familiar. Foster children lose much of their support systems just in time to face the overwhelming challenges of the adult world. Their lives to this point have been turbulent; many have moved through multiple placements before leaving the system. Many youth want to leave a system that has treated them poorly, bounced them around and maintained restrictive rules during their teen years. When they are emancipated on their eighteenth birthdays, as many are, most want nothing more to do with the system. They often immediately disassociate from their families and relationships, and from their therapy for mental health issues. It is well-documented that foster youth have high rates of homelessness, substance abuse, unwanted pregnancy, and criminal activity, and this correlates with the elimination of support that happens when someone ages out of the system. The 2008 Casey Family Programs report states,

> While there are stories about how child welfare services have helped youth succeed, the limited data on the outcomes of many youth who age out consistently paint a grim picture. Youth who age out are less likely than their peers in the general population to achieve academic milestones, including high school graduation and postsecondary education, that signal the foundations of self-sufficiency. These youth are less likely to be employed and, even when they are employed, are more likely to be in jobs that do not pay a living wage. They are more likely to

experience violence, homelessness, mental illness, and other poor health outcomes. They are more likely to be incarcerated, to abuse substances, and to experience early parenthood out-of-wedlock ("Improving outcomes for older youth in foster care." 2008).

Our purpose should be to create systems and programs which provide avenues of success and invest in our youth. It has been my experience that youth in foster care who have more normalized teenage experiences, such as being allowed to get a driver's license, to date, and to attend social events, are often much more willing to remain in foster care, complete high school, and achieve some level of secondary education.

As we address the challenges of older youth it is imperative to ask ourselves if what we are doing is working. How can we create connections at all points of contact—when our children come into our homes, and when they leave? If interconnectivity is as essential to our success and happiness as the food that nurtures us, how can we make our connections as strong and enduring as possible?

*Connection in Practice: Diversity, Peer Pressure, and Limits*

My paternal grandfather and his two brothers opened and ran a plumbing business together their entire lives. My grandfather was a kind, giving man; during the Depression, he allowed people without homes to live in rental properties he owned, for free. He was a quiet man with unwavering ethics and a strong Christian faith. When he developed circulation problems and lost his leg, I remember bringing my first foster child to his house, where he got on the floor to play with the child.

I know that these early, generational demonstrations of the importance of connection have shaped me and my family, as have my husband's experiences. We have always viewed life as an exercise in connection, not isolation. Jim and I believe that true religion is about service. James 1:27 says, "True religion is ministering to orphans and widows," and in many ways we have moved into a time of our life when we are serving the latter. Our family continues to grow, but in different ways. Jim's mother has come to live with us. The branches of our family grow as our children marry and have children of their own. We are in a unique position, now, to consider how the family we built shaped our children, how they have launched, and how they have begun to create their own lives in the world. And, as I look back to the photograph on my desk, I see a dozen ongoing narratives—the stories of how our children have made their way, leaning on Jim, me, and each other for essential support and intertwining their individual paths with the others in our family.

*The Power of Difference*

Speaking with my son Eric one afternoon, I ask him about how our way of life shaped his perceptions of the world. "I think the best part of growing up in a family like ours is learning to manage all of the personalities and having a variety of people to do things with," he says. "Every kid brought something new, sometimes good and sometimes not so good. It was unique in that I definitely had a different perspective growing up than most other people I know. I think having a wider variety of experience has helped me learn how manage people and personalities. Looking at the backgrounds of the some of the children that came into our house really helped me to learn sympathy and how to treat people as individuals based on their needs."

All of the children in our initial "core" family seemed to step into roles that were shaped by their experiences in a diverse and close-knit family. Dimitri, our oldest, assumed a role model position early on, but he was able to do it in a way that wasn't obnoxious. The other boys were proud of him for being their older brother, rather than jealous, and in turn, Dimitri didn't lord it over anyone. He was the valedictorian of his high school, and he went on to earn a Lily scholarship, an Indiana-based scholarship granted to bright students to keep them in state for college. Eric's role in the family was one of energy; he worked hard to make everything fun, to the point that we began to call him the "Social Director." Ivan, a middle child, gravitated toward the younger children, and because of his quiet nature, people—and now our grandchildren—tend to feel safe with him. Our youngest biological child, Alex, has always had an ability to remain emotionally regulated. He never seems to get fazed; rather, he does what he thinks is right, regardless of popular opinion, and he rarely holds a grudge. Each of our children has a distinct personality, but I can see how their role in a group, in the system of our family, brought out their essential skills and traits.

In our diversity, we were able to acknowledge difference, to support each child where he was coming from. There wasn't a "right" way to be, but rather a group acknowledgement of difference. I remember a school term when all of the boys, except for DeShawn, brought home straight As and Bs. DeShawn had always struggled in school, and this was the first quarter in which he had passed all of his classes. As a family, we went out to dinner to celebrate—not the straight As, but DeShawn's success. Our family culture was about recognizing and celebrating effort, even if our efforts and successes did not all look the same.

### The Importance of Peer Pressure

Having a family with so many diverse personalities, ages, home cultures, and backgrounds was a relational blessing, and the sense of interdependence and support also led to positive peer pressure. The strong and consistent relationships in our family have directly affected behavior. The connections that each child forged with the others supported positive behavior and forward momentum, and helped to enforce the choice to do right. Essentially, we were creating an in-crowd within our own home, one that helped to encourage behaviors that aligned with our family's values. As Szalavitz & Perry (2010) write, this kind of crowd mentality, so often associated with negative behavior in the teen years, can actually foster healthier relationships and greater empathy:

> Research that has followed teenagers into adulthood finds that those who follow the crowd tend to be healthier than those who ignore it. Adolescents who care about how other people see them have more friends, better relationships with their families, better grades—and more empathy. Those who don't worry

much about their peers' opinions are the ones who are likely to pull *others* into misbehavior....Programs to prevent risky teen behaviors that work to any extent at all recognize this. Rather than trying to fight peer influence, they attempt to use it positively...Instead of grouping troubled teens together, effective programs work to keep them in the community and place them in situations where youth who are doing well can serve as role models...Because ultimately, constantly resisting group pressures—especially for teens—is like resisting sleep (p. 189).

By creating a family group that promoted values of loving support, responsibility, and acceptance, we were encouraging each child toward positive decision-making. This kind of positive peer pressure within the family proved to be much more effective than using external consequences or punishments to address behaviors. Of course, as parents, there are times when we must apply external consequences, such as the elimination of certain privileges. However, many foster and adopted children have lost so much that taking things away is not effective. If we continuously provide artificial external consequences for behavior for older teens, they don't move to the process of making their own right choices, but continue to be dependent on outside forces, such as the police and the court system, to keep them on the right track. Earning privileges, such as computer time, phones, and cars, is a much more effective way to approach external consequences, but ultimately, our goal should be to help young adults internalize the desire to make the right choice because of their values and the relationships in their life. I want my children (now young adults) to choose to do right because it is the right thing to do, because of the significant relationships in their lives, including God, and because of their desire to be successful in life and relationships. This choice is much easier to make in a family community that encourages, supports, and celebrates doing right.

As a parent and as a caregiver, I often see working with older teens as providing a net as they walk a tightrope. They are going to fall, but the parent and the family become the nets that will catch them, talk with them about what went wrong, and help them back on to the tightrope. The freedom to fall allows them to learn and grow from their mistakes, and to eventually get back on the tightrope of life to try again. All of my children have certainly made mistakes. They have fallen off their tightropes, and done things I didn't approve of. However, as I watched from the ground, offering support, love, and the knowledge that they are still a part of our interconnected family, they have climbed back onto their tightropes, tried again, and continued to become young people I am very proud of.

*Limits*

As our family continues to grow and move forward, we are no longer adopting children. We always adopted for permanence, rather than for growing our family; we adopted when it was in the best interests of the child. I see now, looking back at the wake of the work we have done, how our core family is forming, how some of our children are more firmly part of our day-to-day life. The realization that Dimitri, Allen, DeShawn, Eric, Ivan, Alex, and Louis have come to form our core family has led me to make decisions about limits, to ascertain that we are not sacrificing those relationships. As helpers we only have the capacity to nurture a finite number of relationships, and now we are choosing to prioritize our core family, to watch it grow and expand on its own.

And the work of launching our children continues as they leave the home. I think of Louis, our youngest adopted child. Though many of our children left home to go to college, staying connected in the ways we most often envision—parents' weekend, care packages, holidays at home—Louis did not want to live in the dorm. Instead, he attended a community college in Fort Wayne, living with some friends from our church. It was a difficult year for him, and he came home often. The next two years, he went to live with two of my adult children, Dimitri and Ivan, in Indianapolis, where he attended college. He had our financial and emotional support, and continued connection to our family. Slowly he forged a path that was uniquely his own. I imagine him, in another world, not adopted but in older youth services, moving into a state apartment at eighteen, and then on his own at twenty, and I see a much different life for Louis, one that would have taken from my kind, loving son the essential support, security, and ability to move at his own pace that he needed. DeShawn, similarly, has struggled with his move out of the home, trying community college and eventually becoming the father to two children. And yet, DeShawn is a perfect example of how our connectivity sustains us. Even as his behaviors have often been difficult to understand, the unconditional nature of my love for him is fueled by the knowledge that it is only through relationships that we thrive. Indeed, his children's maternal families have come to be a part of our family as well.

In our proverbial family photograph, in other words, the people we love continue to crowd in, throwing their arms around each other in welcome.

*Toward a Stronger System*

As a parent, as a trainer for the initial Ansell-Casey Life Skills Assessment, and as someone who spent five years overseeing an independent living skills training program in the early 1990s, I am well aware of the challenges youth face as they transition out of foster care. Though the original intent of these independent living programs was to support youth, they don't make sense for every child, and they often mean moving youth from supportive homes into a lonely, unsupported independence. For youth who may be aging out without a supportive family to begin with, the path to "successful" independent living is often paved with workbooks—activities and resources that are aimed to teach youth valuable skills, like money management and how to locate housing. But we don't learn to care for our children through a workbook; we don't understand the ins and outs of supporting ourselves from an afternoon workshop. Very few eighteen year olds are able to live with no family to support them, and this is even less realistic for youth who have experienced significant trauma and transitions.

Some see foster parents as merely caretakers. This role may be true for some. But because of the pervasive negative reputation of the child welfare system, many very good people with genuine hearts for teens are reluctant to foster. Foster parents with the right motives and love are therapeutic in their role with teens, and valuable to both the child welfare system and the community as a whole for the significant impact that they make on our valuable youth.

In 2011, the American Humane Society published a report in their *Protecting Children* publication by Karen Jarboe and Jen Agosti (2011) that detailed a 2008-2010 program in California. Nine counties participated in an overhaul of their Independent Living Programs, and identified key outcomes that are necessary to give youth "permanency for a lifetime." These included ensuring love and belonging; empowering youth to take charge of their lives and futures; and providing youth with what they need to live, love, learn, and work (Agosti & Jarboe, 2011).

In order to advocate for those outcomes, we must be aware of the potentially life-changing benefits of allowing youth to remain in foster care and foster homes through high school graduation. Encouraging foster parents to remain as the youth's support system is critical for the success of youth. We also need to teach our children the skills of daily living, which many children have never been intentionally taught, and require that knowledge-sharing from the foster parents of older teens. Money Management may be a valuable skill, but soft skills are those that sustain us—how to keep a relationship; the importance of family; how to communicate your feelings to the people that you love. It's true that as our children become adults, they do need to learn how to successfully live apart from us, but we teach them a fallacy if we teach them that they never have to be dependent on anyone—and they lose the opportunity for a lifelong relationship each time they resist or are robbed of those connections. As Perry & Szalavtiz (2010) write, "We live our lives in relationships. Shy or outgoing, rich or poor, famous or obscure—whoever we are, without connection, we are empty…From the moment of conception to the end of life, we each engage in a unique dance of connection…inevitably shaped by those around us." To help our children to live successfully is to help them live in relationships, and to begin to create systems that support our ineluctable connectivity and all of the opportunities for love that connectivity provides.

# CHAPTER SIX

## THROUGH A TRAUMA LENS: TOWARD A NEW PARADIGM FOR WORKING WITH TRAUMATIZED CHILDREN

Through these stories, through the experiences of my family and the information I have gathered through research, I hope that reader has gained some new ideas and a sense of solidarity and identification—the knowledge that others have walked this challenging and infinitely rewarding path with traumatized children. Ultimately, my greatest hope is for hope itself—that these stories have provided a sense of all of the potential that exists for these children and their families.

Beginning to view children through a trauma lens is a significant paradigm shift. Our world, and most of the systems within it, are behaviorally oriented. But, as research demonstrates, and as I hope this book has illustrated, the behavior of children who have lived in complex trauma cannot be changed by reasoning, lecturing, or correcting. The frontal cortex, awash in cortisol, is not functioning at a normal developmental level, and before we can expect attachment and reasoning, we have to foster an environment of safety and healing.

This approach of creating a safe and healing environment before attempting to transform a child's behavior—which I enjoy calling my "Mary Poppins approach—firm but kind"—is often seen as counterintuitive. As I provide firm structure for a child, others often view me—and tell me—that I am "inflexible." As I respond in a kind, gentle manner to children, even as they misbehave, the same voices deem me "loosey-goosey" or "way too nice." The approach that I have advocated for throughout this book involves providing structure and then enforcing that structure in a kind, relational manner. The family environment should be one in which the family members take pleasure in each other's company through fun and loving interactions. Creating such an environment is possible when I understand behavior to be the result of trauma, rather than directed at me or reflective of my parenting. This approach is both what I have found to be effective experientially, and also the approach supported by contemporary research.

In this final chapter, I'll discuss the groundbreaking potential of shifting our focus from behavior to trauma. I'll address some of the harder questions about the impact of fostering and adopting on the birth family, and share more about how our family has been ultimately shaped by our experiences. Finally, I'll talk about some of the ways that those of us already working within the new paradigm can continue our work without the anger, burnout, and exhaustion that so often characterizes direct service. There is much work to be done, and my hope is that we can move forward together, with new tools and a shared vision for a better future.

*The Trauma Paradigm and Systems*

One of the most fundamental ways to create change for children in the system is to advocate for changing the system itself. When I teach workshops on trauma-informed care, many of the participants remark about the need for trauma-informed training in all of the systems that touch traumatized children. Much concern is raised by these Masters-level participants who work with traumatized children about the systems in which they work, the courts, the schools, child welfare, and the families in which the children live. All of these systems are important elements of the child's team, yet they do not receive trauma-informed training, nor do they utilize a trauma-informed approach.

While many agencies are beginning to see the value of developing trauma-informed systems and utilizing a trauma-informed approach, many continue to operate from a corrective, behavioral approach to staff and clients. The most unfortunate result of this approach within the child welfare system is that until we begin to understand the impact of trauma on the brain and the effectiveness of a trauma-informed approach for healing, many children will continue to be shifted from system to system. And continuing that cycle means exacerbated trauma; as Perry and Szalavitz (2010) write, "Families unfortunate enough to encounter the mental health, juvenile justice, foster care, and child welfare systems repeatedly discover that these systems create and replicate the chaos, threat, humiliation, trauma, and attachment disruptions that brought their children into these systems in the first place" (p. 302).

One of the greatest services we can provide for the children we work with is to recognize that the most effective trauma work is done when we're working as a team. Certainly, a multidisciplinary team with a trauma-informed approach is ideal. So much of the time in an individual case, the foster care agency doesn't know what the therapist is working on, who doesn't know what the school is working on, who doesn't know what the home-based person is working on, who doesn't know what the visitation person is working on, and so on. This lack of communication means that the support is erratic and the child is being denied an opportunity to receive much more effective care through a congruent treatment plan. When there are multiple people who can share their knowledge and detective work, and who can also help to make sure that a plan is in place for how to handle the behavioral manifestations of trauma, a child stands the best chance of being well-supported.

Indiana has made some strides toward creating a comprehensive interdisciplinary team by instituting what are called Child and Family Team Meetings, which bring together multiple service providers. Ideally, the team should include everyone who is working with the family, but for different reasons, many times the team does not include all of the service providers. Often the foster parents themselves are not included. If there are providers the family doesn't prefer, then it is important to determine why, and to find someone the family feels more comfortable with, if necessary. It is important to consider that everyone on a team of service providers is a professional, including the foster parent and the birth parent, and that the child has a voice as well.

Imagine if the systems and organizations that rule the lives of children in child welfare begin to recognize the value of a trauma-informed approach! Clients and staff will experience an organizational culture that supports staff and clients and creates a climate of trust, open communication, and a sense that staff and clients are walking their journeys together. This culture will offer staff and clients opportunities for continued growth in a supportive emotional and relational climate. One day, I hope we will be a system that is able to look at individual needs; where decisions are made as a multidisciplinary team, rather than by a single caseworker or judge; where children themselves have input in their futures; and where everyone works collaboratively toward the same goals. In a world where everyone is on the same page and seeking to address the trauma and needs behind behaviors, we can provide children with a sense of safety and self.

*Anger*

For those who have lived with a child who has experienced complex trauma, or who have worked in a system or organization that promotes fear, anger is a common emotion. Fear is both a result and a cause of trauma. A work environment, a system, or a family that operates from a fear-based, corrective approach is often full of anger, which does not promote growth. A family with an acting-out, trauma-filled child often shifts to a fear-based system. The family members seek to regain family homeostasis by acquiescing to the demands of the child and "walking on eggshells" to minimize outbursts. Often, this breeds increased anger toward the child and the way the child is behaving. Other families may attempt to regain control through an approach of threats, punishments, and increased anger outbursts. Anger is pervasive in many foster/adoptive families. Some of the child's behaviors create valid feelings of anger, such as when a child who hurts another child. But much of the adult's anger is an underlying fear with many sources, such as fear of failure, fear of loss, and fear of reputation.

Anger and fear are inextricably linked—consider how impossible it is to separate those two emotions in the previous paragraph alone! In order to effectively address the anger, the foster/adoptive parent has to identify the source of the fear. All of us have triggers from our own experiences of feeling wounded. It takes self-awareness and self-reflection, to determine these triggers. It is also helpful to have safe people to help us through this process. The triggers will remain, but knowledge and awareness of them lessen their intensity.

As we begin to recognize our triggers, we can view the child's behavior through the child's trauma and needs, rather than our need for others to see us as good parents. This perspective greatly lessens our emotional response to the child's behavior. Often, the best work we can do for a child is to work with the birth/foster/adoptive parents to identify and acknowledge their own triggers. As we become more aware of our triggers, then our automatic response to a child's behavior is first sifted through our self-awareness of that trigger, and then through our understanding of the child's trauma.

Consider the example of a child who acts out and how the scenario might be addressed through a trauma lens: In viewing the child's behavior, the parent is seeing a child who has experienced trauma, who has certain fear triggers. The parent then responds in a way to calm those fears and reduce emotional intensity; the parent facilitates a feeling of safety, rather than responding in a punitive or negative way. The parent's calm response to the child's need stops the cyclical nature of punitive responses, which could run both parent and child up the anger ladder. As the child escalates, the parent instead becomes what scholar Julie Alvarado refers to as "low and slow." This intentional response reduces increasing anger. The trauma vortex that would have been created from the parent's strong reaction, and the subsequent trauma for the child are avoided, as is the chain reaction of compounding responses and heightened intensity.

I spoke earlier in this book about emotional regulation, which is synonymous to the "low and slow" approach to ending anger. My own knowledge about the importance of avoiding anger was hard won. One Christmas morning, all of our kids had opened their gifts, but our two older girls had retreated to their room, seemingly unappreciative of what they had received. I picked up the discarded gifts from the living room floor, and knocked on their door; I don't remember the words I used, but the hurt look on their faces has stayed with me. The stress, exhaustion, and anger that led to that interaction had only created more hurt. Over time, I began to regulate my emotions and see how a calm response was infinitely more effective.

I also gained much of my ability to regulate my emotions through prayer. For foster/adoptive families who deal with anger and fear on a daily, even moment-to-moment basis, I would encourage continued self-work. By continuing to take a trauma-informed approached to both the child's behaviors and one's own triggers, the destructive and exponential effects of anger can be avoided, leaving more room for the fun and warm interactions that hold families and groups together.

*Avoiding Burnout*

Burnout and vicarious trauma, although often used interchangeably, have different sources and definitions. Burnout is caused by institutional stresses. It is a result of the general psychological stress of working with challenging children, often within a system that provides little support. Vicarious trauma, on the other hand, is a traumatic reaction or response to the child's trauma. As foster/adoptive parents, little can be done to eliminate or even reduce vicarious trauma. The child comes into our home with his trauma intact; it is a piece of who he is. Our response to it, our self-protection, is what we have control over. Issues that lead to burnout also seem to be out of one's control or ability to impact. But there are perhaps more ways to manage burnout and the impact of vicarious trauma than we realize.

Prior to fostering and/or adopting, it is imperative that parents identify their support system. It is helpful for these potential support systems to seek out knowledge and information about the needs and issues of traumatized children. The people who make up these support systems should also be committed to specific support tasks: childcare, meal preparation, laundry, supportive listening, and so on. Many people cannot parent children with the needs of foster and adoptive children, but they can be part of the support system around that family. These people might include our extended family, our church family, and friends in our community or extended community. Often, however, other foster/adoptive parents have the greatest understanding of the children's needs, and become the most significant supporters and resources. For foster/adoptive parents, identifying supporters and support systems is often an ongoing and consuming process—it is clear that support is essential, but it can be challenging to identify those support systems. To avoid burnout and create sustainable systems, parents must keep looking, with purpose and intention, for those who can help them to create a web of lasting support.

At one point in our fostering career, I had a case manager who was very involved with the young man I had in my home. While the case manager's work with this young man was important, perhaps the greatest gift he gave me was in passing—he told me of another foster family who lived just down the road from us. The foster mother and I became fast friends and great supporters to one another. Although we have both moved across distances and neither of us fosters any longer, we are still, and will always be, good friends. Another great gift in my life was a woman from my church, who viewed her ministry as supporting our family. She came to our house every day after school, staying there until I came home from work. She loved our children; she cleaned our house; she started dinner. Her support was immeasurable, and when our family moved I was saddened to lose the support she had provided. Soon enough, however, new foster parents and other community members entered our lives and began again to weave that net of support and love around us.

I relate these anecdotes because, though seemingly small, the actions of our support system gave us the strength to move through and around burnout and vicarious trauma. A wide network, including my sisters and in-laws, supported me, challenged me, taught me, and loved me, and because of that support, I was able to love the children I was supporting, even through the most challenging moments and situations. Finding a community of people who understand our challenges is critical to our success in remaining effective with children, and, on a simple level, to our happiness.

*Grace, Forgiveness, Unconditional Love, and Boundaries*

In Chapter Five, I spoke about my son DeShawn, who came into our home when he was sixteen and whom we adopted the following year, and how my unconditional love and focus on the relationship between us trumps the behaviors that I sometimes disagree with. I'd like to talk about DeShawn once more, since he has been such an important example to me of unconditional love. My

Mama Bear comes out when someone is critical of my children—all who are now, of course, young adults. When DeShawn struggles with maintaining a job, or encounters legal trouble, I often encounter criticism from those voices who would advocate that I disown him. But he, just like my successful sons, is my son and I love him. He has taught me many important things about unconditional relationships. He has taught me about grace, forgiveness, and unconditional love, but also about setting boundaries.

I don't know a lot of DeShawn's first fifteen years of his life, but over time I have begun to gain insight into his childhood, into the minimal supervision and the transient nature of the people who were in and out of his home. As the picture of DeShawn's childhood becomes clearer, I am increasingly amazed at what a good dad he is, even though he did not have a dad until he came into our home at the age of sixteen. DeShawn has taught me that his need for a committed mom and dad is more important than anything material in my life, but has also taught me about boundaries. I have learned to lock up items I don't want taken, such as my jewelry. I had to make the decision that he couldn't live with us when I found that he was bringing pornography into our home. Even with him leaving, we have attempted to stay connected. I support and encourage him and, at times, help him financially. We pay for his phone so that I know that I can be connected to him. And I have learned about grace—he has not always been as involved in the lives of his children as he is now; I give him grace and rejoice in the time he now spends with them and how much they love him.

Grace is *their needs* and not *my needs*. Grace is forgiving, even when we haven't seen remorse. Unconditional love is loving even when we don't receive in return. I love unconditionally not because it is easy, but because it is what my child needs.

And, when I need a reminder of the essential nature of grace, forgiveness, boundaries, and unconditional love, I look again at DeShawn. My intentional grace and forgiveness are, I believe, finally working. He is now engaged to a beautiful woman, working full-time, and still caring for his children. When he behaves in ways that I don't support, I set firm boundaries and I remind him that, no matter what,

I love him. And, in return, he is now a son who is kind and loving to us and others, who is breaking the trauma cycle and becoming a father to his children in a way he himself perhaps never thought possible.

*The Impact on Birth Children: Important Questions and Considerations*

The process of writing this book has meant taking a close look at the way that Jim and I chose to live. Sometimes that has meant asking hard questions, ones without clear or easy answers, such as the impact of fostering on my birth children. Without question, our young children, both in our birth and core family, were often therapeutic to our foster children. For example, when we fostered teen girls, who had often been very hurt by adults, our biological children were very young. Holding and loving our babies gave these teen girls an outlet for expressing their love. However, when we look at the question of impact from the other side of the table, the waters become a little muddy. What was the impact on our birth children, and was it positive or negative?

This is a question that is often posed to me, and when I ask the question of my three birth sons, they reply that they knew nothing different, so have nothing to compare it to; we started fostering when my oldest son was two years old. My birth sons have reflected that they feel they have more compassion than most people their age. I believe it also provided for them an experience of cultural and socio-economic diversity, as well as insight into the effects of the drug culture. My sons say that they would never want to have lived differently, especially when it comes to their adopted brothers, whom they consider brothers in the fullest extent of the word. They are proud of our family, of our family's ministry, and of the lives that our family impacted. Still, I would be remiss to say that I thought there were no ramifications.

I struggle at times wondering if we made the right choice in raising our biological children with foster and adopted children. I believe my birth sons experienced some bullying from the some of the foster youth. My time and attention was also less for each of them because they had to share me with so many others. I often ask the question of other people's birth children—*What is it like for you to be birth child in a foster home?* Most respond positively, seeing the contributions they have made to changed lives. Some resent the time that fostering takes away from their parents. Others resent the ongoing displacement in their home. Although we tried to minimize such displacement—the moving of bedrooms, the missing of activities—this still sometimes occurred in our home.

I don't think the question of whether to foster with birth children in the home has a clear or definitive answer. I think that it needs to be a personal decision, based on the strengths of the core family. Fostering and adopting indisputably impact the children in the home, perhaps even more than the parents, but this impact can be a positive, rewarding experience, instilling in the child compassion for others and a desire to make a difference in the world. I hope that this has been the impact on my birth and adopted children.

I would like to share an essay that my son, Dimitri, wrote as part of a high school autobiography assignment for his Junior year English class. I think his words do much to reveal the impact of fostering and adoption on our family, regardless of whether or not there is a clear answer to whether or not the decisions we made were the "right" ones:

*My family is a foster family. That is a family that opens up its doors to children of dysfunctional homes. Currently I have one foster brother who is 14; I also have one adopted brother who is 13. Both aren't just roommates – they are brothers at heart. Over the years my family has had upwards of 40 children walk into our house. Some were old; others young; some became close, while others were but a one night stay. I also have two biological brothers, age 12 and 9. I am the oldest, the holder of the coveted "biggest room." Eric and Allen are budding football stars (as they claim). Allen plays at quarterback and safety. Eric's position is linebacker. Ivan and Eric have recently taken up wrestling, the high school sport of my father. Both flirt with the heavyweight division. Alex, Ivan, and Eric all have a love for soccer. Allen, Alex and Eric are avid basketball players. Everyone bicycles, some more than others. With forty siblings, stories alone could fill a library. One foster sister's story was on a talk show and was the* subject of a book. Another ran away at least 1,412 times (a slight exaggeration). One sibling group stole everything they saw, deftly and unseen. They had helped their mother who was part of a gypsy thief ring. When we came home from a fast food place, we learned their skill by finding tons of chicken nuggets in the sleeves of their coats. One of my former foster brothers has grown to six foot four, 350 pound plus size. One more foster sister lied consistently about nearly everything. Not that she was the only eloquent liar. And who can forget the infamous "chili incident" where an entire vat of chili was found dripping from the kitchen ceiling. The stains can be seen to this day. The asylum will continue to procure new and more unbelievable stories, I am sure.

     My foster siblings have influenced me in a unique way that no one else could. They have exposed me to a society not often found in our secluded town. There have been nearly forty young people who have crossed our threshold, each with their own set of needs and issues. Each brings a unique heritage to share. Every child has a fact of life to teach. The Hispanic and Black children taught me about diversity. Teen drug and alcohol addicts showed me the consequences of bad choices. Children with attachment disorders showed me that one bad relationship can poison all others. Crack babies are a reminder that one's choices affect more people than just one oneself. Abused kids revealed the sickening truth about America's "ideal" society. These children didn't always come from a Gary slum like some people would want to think. They came from houses where the American dream was a reality – homes of wealthy doctors, well-to-do businessmen and Joe Average families. These children gave me the knowledge of the true America. One child with AIDS showed me how terrible that disease truly was. She will not live to grow old. I have seen how mental diseases are just as devastating. These are all things I knew before these people came into my life. Why are these people's object lessons so important to me? I already knew such terrible tragedies existed. But the firsthand sight of these people, their lives and woes, brought a bland statistic on black and white paper to life. It is one thing to know. It is another to understand. The knowing was somehow less real to me than seeing children with problems in person.

     Todd was only in my home for eight months, and so while I would call all of my foster brothers family, he was more of a visitor to me. Even so, in those eight months, I learned more about myself than in any period of time as a young adult. My family has fostered children in need of a home for all of my life. I learn something new from each child that comes into our house, whether they stay only for a short time or long enough that they become just as much a part of my family *as my biological brothers. But Todd was especially world-changing to me. He came as a small eleven year old, scarred from abuse and broken attachments. He was at once difficult and rewarding. Todd arrived at just at the right time in my life and taught me immensely about what kind of person I was, not only when successful, but also in my failures.*

*I have always said that I want to have a career working with children, and Todd helped me realize what I had the ability to accomplish. I worked with him on school work daily. Soon his grades and behavior improved. I would take him with me to many of my activities and regularly and gradually his violent behavior and depressive moods became less frequent. This gave me confidence in myself and hope. Todd helped me to realize the priceless value that comes with helping others.*

*Todd also forced me both to learn how to handle failure and how to ascertain knowledge from it. I was not accustomed to failure, whether it be in academics, sports, or at home. With Todd, however, there were many failures. The years of physical abuse left him untrusting and mentally volatile. As Todd and I became closer to success, his damaged instincts made him push away from me and lash out at others. His grades plummeted and he became violent at home. I was angry and disappointed, but soon I learned how determined I could be to not give up. But his behavior was quickly degrading. He began striking my parents and brothers and cursing at them. I grew more angry, asking myself bitterly why my family and I give so much and receive only pain in return. But this made me learn how to forgive and how to continue to love. I realized the answer to my own question: all people are worth helping, and giving is its own reward. Eventually Todd's violence went to school also, and he had to be moved. But the eight months that he was in my life changed it inexplicably and permanently.*

*There are so very many hurting children like Todd that are not yet lost. I believe strongly that every child has a hope for a good life in the future. I want to help children like Todd, who have had such a terrible past, find a hopeful new life.*

*We have a full house, some might say. Others might tell us we are simply nuts. But we have a good time and two good parents to keep us in line, whomever "us" might be. To the person who has a simple 1.7 child family that can barely survive an adolescent, I can only laugh. Perfect homes are boring ones; they ignore the beauty of chaos. My family helps children. A perfect family with a perfect life is a selfish way to live. The gift of a family, of acceptance, gives back. Maybe one*

*Chinese proverb put it best, "Tell me and I'll forget/Show me and I may remember/Involve me and I'll understand. I was involved, and the same knowledge I knew before now changed my life. These people shaped who I am."*

*What Does All This Mean?*

The four tenets of trauma-informed care, as described by the National Network of Hospital-Based Violence Intervention Programs, are *safety, emotional management, loss,* and *future*. Safety is the key to the healing process; neither children nor adults can change until they feel safe, and the process of healing begins within a safe environment with people who feel safe to the individual. When we consider safety for children, we have to consider our approach, and how we might create an environment for children that feels physically, psychologically, and emotionally safe. This environment is created by adults who manage their emotional reactions, remaining emotionally regulated even during times of the child's high emotion.

Loss, as we have discussed, is a significant factor for every foster and adopted child, but frequently is not acknowledged or addressed for children. Most children have experienced multiple losses, yet we minimize or don't acknowledge those losses. As we talk about our own feelings, our own losses, we model for our children that grief and sadness are normal, and expressing our feelings is acceptable. The final tenet, future, is perhaps the most important, because it is the tenet that provides hope for tomorrow. By working with children in a trauma-informed paradigm and helping them to reconcile their past losses and work toward successful futures, we give them the ability to cultivate hope, self-importance, and stories of their own futures that they can walk toward.

Utilizing a trauma-informed paradigm is a strengths-based approach which recognizes the pervasiveness of trauma and is committed to understanding the link between presenting behaviors and symptoms and the individual's trauma history. A trauma-informed approach is one which serves others through a lens of the child's trauma history, and within a framework committed to "do no harm." This approach is one that does not inflict further trauma on the individual, or reactivate past traumatic experiences. This approach, this lens, this paradigm, is one in which the purpose is to assist the child to heal.

A trauma-informed paradigm is one that would revolutionize our families, our communities, our organizations, and our systems. Sometimes, as I teach the workshop to other professionals on Trauma Informed Care, I think, *What if this were the mantra of the world? What if we treated everyone as if they had experienced trauma? What if we were, as a world, a group of people who treated each other with kindness, love, and respect? What if grace, forgiveness, and unconditional love were the currencies that drove our social transactions and relationships?* What an amazing world we would live in. In my spiritual viewpoint, it is what I hope heaven to be.

# References

Agosti, J., & Jarboe, K. (2011). Independent living transformation in California: lessons learned about working with older youth and implications for permanency In *Love and belonging for a lifetime: Youth permanency in Child Welfare* (1 ed., Vol. 26, p. 15). American Humane Society.

Boss, P. (1999). *Ambiguous loss: Learning to live with unresolved grief.* Cambridge, MA: Harvard University Press.

Bunim, J. (2013, July 9). Breakthrough Study Reveals Biological Basis for Sensory Processing Disorders in Kids. *USCF News*. Retrieved April 26, 2014, from http://www.ucsf.edu/news/2013/07/107316/breakthrough-study-reveals-biological-basis-sensory-processing-disorders-kidsi

Casey Family Programs, (2008). *Improving outcomes for older youth in foster care.*

Fahlberg, V. (1991). *A child's journey through placement.* Indianapolis: Perspectives Press.

Friesen, J., Wilder, E. J., Bierling, A., Koepcke, R., & Poole, M. (2000). *The life model; living from the heart Jesus gave you.* Pasadena, CA: Shepherd's House, Inc.

Gulden, H. v., & Sutton, A. (2014). *And you are still you: Developing and maintaining a stable sense of self.* : Lulu.

Karr-Morse, R., & Wiley, M. S. (1997). *Ghosts in the nursery: Tracing the roots of violence.* New York: The Atlantic Monthly Press.

Kline, C. B. (Writer) (2013). After tragedy, young girl shipped west on 'orphan train' [Radio series episode]. In *Weekend Edition Sunday*. NPR. Retrieved from http://www.npr.org/2013/04/14/176920218/qhttp://www.npr.org

/2013/04/14/176920218/after-tragedy-young-girl-shipped-west-on-orphan-train

Kranowitz, C. S. (2005). *The out-of-sync child: recognizing and coping with sensory processing disorder* (Rev. and updated ed.). New York: A Skylight Press Book/A Perigee Book.

Levine, P. A., & Kline, M. (2007). *Trauma through a child's eyes.* Berkeley, CA: North Atlantic Books.

MN Adopt, (n.d.). *Understanding ambiguous loss: Fact sheet.* Retrieved from website: https://mnadopt.org/Factsheets/Understanding Ambiguous Loss.pdf

Perry, B., & Szalavitz, M. (2010). *Born for love: Why empathy is essential--and endangered.* New York: HarperCollins.

Perry, B., & Szalavitz, M. (2006). *The boy who was raised as a dog and other stories from a child psychiatrist's notebook: What traumatized children can teach us about loss, love, and healing.* New York, NY: Basic Books.

Perry, B. (n.d.). *Attachment: The first core strength.* Retrieved from http://teacher.scholastic.com/professional/bruceperry/attachment.htm

Sensory Processing Disorder Foundation | Research, Education and Advocacy. (n.d.).*Sensory Processing Disorder Foundation | Research, Education and Advocacy.* Retrieved April 26, 2014, from http://www.spdfoundation.net/

Spitz, R.A. (1946). Hospitalism; A follow-up report on investigation described in volume I, 1945. The Psychoanalytic Study of the Child, 2, 113-117.

Spitz, R. A. (1965). The First Year of Life. A Psychoanalytic Study of Normal and Deviant Development of Object Relations. New York: International Universities Press, Inc.

Straugh, B. (2003). *The primal teen.* New York: Doubleday.

The orphans trains [Television series episode]. (1995). In *The*

*American experience*. PBS Home Video. Retrieved from http://www.pbs.org/wgbh/amex/orphan/index.html

Twomey, S. (2010, January). *Phineas gage: Neuroscience's most famous patient*. Retrieved from http://www.smithsonianmag.com/history-archaeology/Phineas-Gage-Neurosciences-Most-Famous-Patient.html

Van der Kolk, B. (Performer) (2002). The secret life of the brain [Television series episode].

# ABOUT THE AUTHORS

Nancy Fisher initially began working in the child welfare system as a foster parent in 1985. In 1991, she became a foster parent trainer for the State and provided pre-service and in-service training for foster parents until 2003. In 1995, she began working for White's Residential and Family Services where she worked extensively with foster parents. She then developed the post adoption services program for Northern Indiana, developing programs and services for adoptive families. She served as the Director of Adult and Children Services at LifeTouch Ministries and Counseling Center, and now works as a therapist for Family Concern Counseling. She also provides trauma-informed care training to mental health practitioners across the state of Indiana. Nancy and her husband Jim were foster parents for 23 years and adopted four teen boys during their time as foster parents. They also have three biological sons.

Megan Kruse assisted on this project. Her first novel is forthcoming from Hawthorne Books in 2015. Find her at www.megannicolekruse.com.

Made in the USA
Charleston, SC
08 November 2014